FOR EVERY IDLE SILENCE

For Every Idle Silence

Henry J. Hyde

SERVANT BOOKS
Ann Arbor, Michigan

Cover design by Charles Picirilli, Graphicus Corp.
Cover photo by Bruce Weller

Published by Servant Publications, Box 8617, Ann Arbor,
Michigan 48107

ISBN 0-89283-282-7
Printed in the United States of America

88 89 10 9 8 7 6 5 4 3

Not only for every idle word but for every idle silence must man render an account.
—St. Ambrose

*To my wife Jeanne and my family—for
their love and support*

Contents

Acknowledgments

Special thanks are due to the American Enterprise Institute for its generous permission to reprint the text of the debate "Religion and the Constitution."

My deep gratitude to George Weigel, then a fellow of the Woodrow Wilson International Center for Scholars, whose advice on my Notre Dame speech was invaluable. My favorite columnist, Joseph Sobran, and my friend, Phil Nicolaides, reviewed the text and made helpful suggestions.

I am indebeted to Tom Smeeton for his help on the essay on liberation theology.

In preparing my response to the bishops' second draft of their Pastoral Letter on Nuclear Warfare, Philip Lawler was extraordinarily helpful.

My thanks to James Manney of Servant Publications who first suggested this book and whose patience and editorial skills were indispensable.

Last, but certainly not in rank of contribution, Judy Wolverton of my staff provided encouragement and constructive criticism which helped get this book written in the first place.

ONE

Why Has Politics Become So Religious (and Religion So Political)?

T WO INTERRELATED ISSUES loom above all others in the contemporary political scene: the role of religion in politics and the phenomenon of abortion. The 1984 presidential campaign featured a furious debate about religion and religious leaders in politics. At stake was the White House—the greatest prize our political system can offer. The debate was often partisan, but the underlying issues were ones that have often been raised in the past twenty years and will undoubtedly be raised again—loudly and insistently—in the years ahead. This book is largely concerned with those issues.

This book is also concerned with abortion—the most intense value-laden debate in contemporary politics. The struggle over legalized abortion is bitter. Many politicians would like to run away from the issue. They cannot. Many voters wish the abortion issue would go away. It won't. Legalized abortion, with its manifold consequences and implications, is playing an increasingly important role in national politics. It is the paramount issue in what I consider to be the decisive conflict of our day—the struggle over values in our national life. There are forces at work to sterilize society from any hint of religious activity or sentiment, and the abortion issue is frequently the focus of their efforts.

This fact touched me personally in 1977 at the height of a court battle over the constitutionality of the so-called Hyde Amendment which barred federal funding for abortion in the Medicaid program. Much to the surprise and consternation of proabortion groups, Congress had passed the amendment in 1976. The American Civil Liberties Union (ACLU), Planned Parenthood, and other plaintiffs who opposed the ban rushed into federal court to challenge its constitutionality. They found a federal judge in Brooklyn, New York, who agreed to enjoin enforcement of the amendment. Senator James Buckley of New York and I appealed and got the U.S. Supreme Court to order the injunction dissolved. The case went back to the Brooklyn court, and in 1977 lawyers on our side and I were grappling with supporters of abortion in a case that would determine whether thousands of unborn children would be permitted to live.

The case was also full of intriguing constitutional questions. One of the most interesting of these, at least in the minds of the ACLU and Planned Parenthood, was the fact that I was a Catholic. They developed a theory that the Hyde Amendment "used the fist of government to smash the wall of separation between church and state by imposing a peculiarly religious view of when a human life begins." To gather support for this theory, the plaintiffs asked to review my mail in order to find expressions of religious sentiment. Partly to avoid a court battle over this demand and partly in the hope that my opponents would learn something, I agreed to let my mail be examined on the condition that my correspondents' identities be kept secret.

So the plaintiffs' lawyers and my lawyers sat down and examined great piles of my mail. They did find expressions of religious sentiment. The ACLU and Planned Parenthood lawyers drew up a large chart. Whenever they found a letter that supported my view on abortion and closed with an expression such as "God bless you," one of the lawyers solemnly checked an appropriate box on the chart with further evidence of a religious conspiracy.

Worse was to come. One evening I attended mass at St. Thomas More Cathedral in Arlington, Virginia, not far from my home in Falls Church. Bishop Thomas Welsh of Arlington was presiding at a mass to pray for the preservation of the lives of the unborn and had invited me to attend. I did so gladly.

Unknown to me and others at the mass, I was followed into church by a private investigator working for the plaintiffs in the Hyde Amendment suit. He took notes. He watched me get up to read the epistle at mass, take communion, and appear to pray. He even followed me to a reception in the church hall afterward where I chatted with other prolife people. The private eye went so far as to write down a famous quotation written on a statue of St. Thomas More, one of my heroes and patron of the cathedral: "I die the king's good servant but God's first."

These observations went into an affidavit that the plaintiffs attempted to introduce in court as yet more evidence of religious conspiracy. They argued that the Hyde Amendment was unconstitutional because its principal sponsor was a devout Catholic who could not separate his religious beliefs from his political activity.

The judge threw out the affidavit. Planned Parenthood and the ACLU ultimately lost their case in 1980 when the United States Supreme Court affirmed the constitutionality of the Hyde Amendment by a narrow 5-4 margin. But the arguments of my courtroom opponents made a deep impression on me. The anger I felt when they tried to disenfranchise me because of my religion has stayed with me. These are dangerous people who make dangerous arguments. Some powerful members of the cultural elites in our country are so paralyzed by the fear that theistic notions might reassert themselves in the official activities of government that they will go to Gestapo lengths to inhibit such expression.

These efforts are revolutionary in the literal sense of the term. They do radical violence to our history and constitution.

A study of our political liberties requires understanding of our historical experience, including the religious beliefs which generated the moral precepts upon which our liberties are based. Judge Robert Bork of the U.S. Court of Appeals in the District of Columbia, in an address entitled "Tradition and Morality in Constitutional Law" (American Enterprise Institute, Washington, D.C.), states that constitutional law has little theory of its own, and therefore is nearly "pathologically lacking in immune defenses against the intellectual fevers of the larger society," which, Judge Bork tells us, results in the law becoming "unstable, a ship with a great deal of sail but a very shallow keel, vulnerable to the winds of intellectual or moral fashion, which it then validates as the commands of our most basic compact." This produces a sort of "constitutional nihilism" where arbitrary judgment takes the place of constitutional text, precedent, tradition, and history.

In the context of today's debate over the proper role of religion in public life, it is startling to recall that Justice William O. Douglas (one of modern liberalism's most heroic figures) spoke for the majority of the Supreme Court in *Zorach v. Clausen* (1951) when he said, "we are a religious people whose institutions presuppose a supreme being."

But this is an unpopular notion today among establishment opinion-molders, and so, yes, there is much to be said about historical tradition in defense of the proper role (I would assert the indispensable role) of religion in politics.

Whether the intentions of the Founding Fathers still provide the sole legitimating guideposts for constitutional analysis or whether, as today's legal climate suggests, the judge's own prepossessions control is a question whose answer has tremendous implications for our liberties.

According to Judge Bork, the privatization of our religious beliefs results in the "thought that individuals are entitled to their moral beliefs but may not gather as a community to express those moral beliefs in law." He asserts that "the major freedom of our kind of society is the freedom to choose to have a public morality."

We can have a "public morality" mindful of the apprehensions of our Jewish brethren that assertions such as "We are a Christian nation" are anathema to them. We can do so and feel perfectly comfortable in an environment of religious pluralism. Indeed, we must do so if freedom of religion is to have any meaning at all. But should the atheist or those hostile to formal religion be able to suppress the legitimate expression of religiously based morality, to invalidate and delegitimize it as somehow contrary to the First Amendment? Does freedom of religion mean freedom from religion? These are questions worth asking, and they require answers.

We owe an important concession to intellectual honesty by admitting that our historical tradition displays a close link between religiously based values and the laws that protect our basic liberties. Whatever merit or utility the arguments for distancing the law from these values might have, they cannot be said to be in keeping with historical tradition, but rather a considerable departure.

One of the most useful commentaries on this subject is that of Professor Harold J. Berman of the Harvard Law School appearing in the *Journal of Law and Religion* (summer 1983), entitled "Religious Foundations of Law in the West: An Historical Perspective" in which he tells us:

> For over eight hundred years, from the late eleventh to the early twentieth century, law in the West was supported by, and in many respects based on, religious beliefs, both Roman Catholic and Protestant. In the twentieth century the intimate connection between the Western legal tradition and the Western religious tradition has been substantially broken.

Many modern legal scholars must consider "quaint" the words of the freethinking Thomas Jefferson, who said that "the only firm basis" of a nation's liberties is "a conviction in the minds of people that their liberties are the gift of God." The same idea was expressed by Jefferson's rival, Alexander Hamilton:

> The sacred rights of mankind are not to be rummaged for among old parchments or musty records. They are written, as with a sunbeam, in the whole volume of human nature, by the hand of the Divinity itself; and can never be erased or obscured by mortal power.

Professor Berman, in pointing out the twentieth century's gradual reduction of traditional religion to the level of a private matter, without public influence on legal development, cites the consequences of this privatization of religion:

1) The fragmentation and disintegration of the law—the law has changed from a coherent whole, a *corpus juris,* into a collection of ad hoc decisions; a "primitive pragmatism" is all the justification used to explain many decisions.

2) The belief that the law grows through an interpretation of the past is no longer valid—"the law is presented as having no history of its own."

3) The view that law is above mere politics has surrendered to the idea that the law is politics; the law is simply current policy with no past and no real future.

Professor Berman sounds an ominous warning when he says:

> The law is becoming more fragmented, more subjective, geared more to expediency and less to morality, concerned more with immediate consequences and less with consistency or continuity. Thus the historical soil of the Western legal tradition is being washed away in the twentieth century, and the tradition itself is threatened with collapse.

These troubling reflections have come to me as I begin my second decade in Congress and my sixteenth year in elective office. I did not come into politics with a great interest in the rather heavy subject of values in public policy. Fittingly enough for a politician, I developed the misgivings I now have in the course of the cut and thrust and compromise of a politician's often unreflective active life. Appropriately enough, the crisis of abortion introduced me to the crisis of church and state.

It happened in 1969. I was a busy member of the Illinois General Assembly dividing my time between the Assembly in Springfield and my law practice in Chicago. I was dimly aware of efforts in other states to liberalize laws that typically made abortion a crime except in cases where the mother's life was at stake. Hawaii had loosened its laws. Well-publicized campaigns to do likewise were underway in Colorado, California, and New York. In keeping with the mood of the day, an assemblyman named Leland Rayson decided to introduce a bill to liberalize abortion laws in Illinois. He was a Democrat who wanted a cosponsor who was Republican, Catholic, and conservative. I was all three, so Rayson asked me to join him. I had not thought much at all about the abortion issue. I promised to think about it and get back to him.

I quickly decided that abortion was something to be resisted strenuously. A book that was particularly helpful at the time was *The Vanishing Right to Live* by Charles Rice. The note of prophetic alarm in the book's title sounds even more loudly today after the holocaust of one and a half million abortions every year since 1973, the quiet acceptance of infanticide, and recently the threat of euthanasia of older people. I led the opposition to Rayson's bill. We defeated it and its progeny in subsequent sessions, until the Supreme Court overrode all state abortion laws in its disastrous *Roe v. Wade* decision in 1973.

I was thus swept into the abortion debate by the circumstances of practical politics. There was, and to a large degree still is, a leadership vacuum on this issue. I became the leading opponent of legalized abortion in the Illinois Assembly largely because most of my colleagues were not at all interested in discussing the issue. Abortion was and is a technical, emotional, and controversial issue. It is what politicians call a "no win" issue—something that will make you enemies no matter what you do.

My prolife leadership on the national level also happened casually, almost by accident. When I went to Congress in 1974, prolife legislators were almost exclusively concerned with gathering support for a constitutional amendment banning abortion. The votes for an amendment were not there then and they still are not there today. Congressmen would cosponsor amendments to the constitution and the bills would be thrown into the drawer to gather dust. There was no real action in Congress. There was almost a resignation to the decision of the Supreme Court that abortion was a legitimate surgical procedure and a birth control option.

In 1976, during the floor debate on the appropriation bill for the Department of Health, Education, and Welfare, a member of Congress named Bob Bauman mentioned to me that the bill contained $50 million to pay for 300,000 Medicaid abortions. He suggested that an amendment striking this money would be appropriate. Bauman, whose political career later came to a tragic end, was known as an outspoken, staunch conservative. He suggested that I introduce the amendment because, as a freshman in Congress, I was an unknown quantity.

Bauman and I scribbled out language for what later became known as the Hyde Amendment. I went forward to the well of the House and offered the amendment on the spot. The Democrat who was managing the bill was outraged. Other members of Congress arose in high dudgeon to denounce the amendment. Others supported me. Almost by accident I ignited a conflagration over abortion that still rages.

It is right that a conflagration rage over abortion. The abortion issue deals with many more questions than the humanity of the preborn. It asks us about duty and love and the nature of suffering and sacrifice in this life. It reminds us that the handicapped, while possibly an emotional and financial drain on families and society, always add to the gross spiritual product of mankind. And abortion asks the fundamental question, "What is man?"

To the believing Christian, man is certainly the object of God's redemptive love. The philosopher Jean-Paul Sartre died on April 15, 1980, having spent his years as an atheist. But in 1980, blind and failing in body, he had remarkable dialogue with his friend Peter Victor. One sentence of that published dialogue, a repudiation of Sartre's entire life, is unforgettable: "I do not feel," Sartre said, "that I am the product of chance, a speck of dust in the universe, but someone who was expected, prepared, prefigured. In short, a being whom only a creator could put here; and this idea of a creating hand refers to God."

One of the saddest postscripts to a human life was written by William Marcy when James K. Polk, having finished his single term as President, started home for Tennessee. Polk was only fifty-four years old then, but the strain of travel was too much for him and on June 15, 1849, he died. Marcy, who had been Polk's Secretary of War, wrote in his diary of his friend, "What shadows we are, what shadows we pursue."

But we need more than the emptiness of that epitaph if we believe in the possibilities of human life, the opportunities and challenges that are at the heart of the human condition. The importance—the sublime importance of every single human life was expressed by Father Anthony Padovano, who wrote: "Tragedies which break our hearts again and again are not more numerous than the healing influences which mend us. More impressive than the brokenness of our hearts is the fact that we have a heart and that it is tender enough to suffer. Even a scar tells us of more than the wound we have sustained; it tells us that we have prevailed. No agony is sufficient to cancel out the fact that a man was born and that life and thought, emotion and choice, love and reason go on inside him."

This world and our lives are characterized by struggle. But the struggle *is* worth the effort. Mary Meehan, one of the most effective writers in defense of the unborn, has reminded us of a more ennobling epitaph than Marcy's shadow, if we summon up our courage and our conscience. She quotes the poet Stephen Spender:

> I think continually of those
> who were truly great. . . .
> the names of those who in their
> lives fought for life,
> Who wore at their hearts the
> fire's centre.
> Born of the sun, they traveled
> a short while toward the sun,
> and left the vivid air signed with
> their honor.

It is that fight for life that those of us who would defend "that tiny atom of humanity surrounded by a woman we call mother" seek to make. May our efforts be worthy of this great cause.

This book reflects certain convictions that I have developed over the years as I have become involved in the abortion crisis and other controversies. I think we are engaged in a fierce debate over values that threaten our democracy. Articulate public officials argue that we should exclude religiously based values from the public arena. The essay "Keeping God in the Closet: Some Thoughts on the Exorcism of Religious Values from Public Life" is my rejoinder to the spokesmen and spokeswomen for this view. They were much in evidence during the 1984 presidential campaign.

The debate published here as "Religion and the Constitution" shows the extent of current church-state controversies. It includes school prayer, tuition tax credits, the public display of religious symbols, the rights of students to meet in public schools to discuss religious topics, and role of the courts in interpreting the First Amendment.

A third essay, "Spiritual Leadership and the Abortion Crisis," discusses abortion in the context of the profound spiritual crisis that is gripping this country. I also set forth my views on how the abortion crisis can be resolved.

"Ethics in Conflict: Quality of Life vs. Sanctity of Life" discusses the profound struggle over ethical values that lies at the heart of the abortion debate.

"Priestly Peacemakers: The Bishops and Nuclear Strategy" reflects my conviction, and that of many of my Congressional colleagues, that some religious reflection on public policy is seriously deficient. This essay is a response to the second draft of the U.S. Catholic bishops' famous pastoral letter on war and peace.

A final essay concerns human rights. This has not been a good century for human rights. They are so thoroughly violated in so many ways that we need to passionately defend them whenever we can.

I have reflected on these questions as a Christian whose career lies in politics. I do not claim that my views are the only legitimate Christian views. To claim this, or even to imply it, would be wrong and also offensive. Rather I believe that I will one day render an account to God for what I did and failed to do about the issues that have caused such deep distress in our national life. I have tried to speak out and exercise my responsibilities as a Christian.

I have always felt greater remorse over sins of omission than of commission—the things we fail to do rather than the things we do. Politicians are not known for their silence. But we often are silent. Like other people, we are silent in the face of injustice. We fail to speak out when we see wrong being done. St. Ambrose warned us: "Not only for every idle word but for every idle silence must man render an account." I have taken this warning as the title for this book. I also take it to heart, and I hope you do too.

TWO

Keeping God in the Closet:
Some Thoughts on the Exorcism of Religious Values from Public Life

The debate over the role of religion and politics reached a crescendo in the 1984 presidential campaign. There were several reasons for this. None of them was predictable, although in hindsight we can see that a storm over the so-called church-state issue has been brewing for many years. Once these forces came together, it was inevitable that religion and politics would become a source of controversy.

The first reason was the ascendency of the Reverend Jesse Jackson to a position of a serious contender for the presidency. Mr. Jackson's campaign upset many prominent Jewish Democrats. He had long been more favorably disposed to the Palestine Liberation Organization and Yassir Arafat than many Jews found acceptable. Their doubts were intensified when Louis Farrakhan, an anti-Semitic black extremist, rose to prominence in Jackson's campaign. Black and Jewish Democrats were also divided over the issue of quotas in employment and other areas. Jews have long opposed the use of quotas, having observed, accurately, that quotas have traditionally been used in other times and places to exclude Jews. The liberal black leadership, on the other hand, strongly supported quotas. These two issues had enough potential to fuel a very serious conflagration between two important elements of the Democratic party.

Another aspect of Mr. Jackson's campaign received less attention from those concerned about the role of religion in politics. Mr. Jackson was an ordained Baptist minister who organized his campaign largely through black churches, used churches to raise money and register supporters, and often used church settings to receive endorsements and endorse other candidates. Religion and politics had seldom been so intimately mixed in American political history.

The campaign also saw the ascendency of conservative Protestant evangelicals who suddenly decided that they would not abandon the political arena to their liberal brethren. Conservative Protestants became interested in many political issues and in the reelection campaign of President Reagan and Vice President Bush. The leader and symbol for this movement was the Reverend Jerry Falwell of the Moral Majority.

President Reagan helped sharpen the problem when he spoke at a prayer breakfast in Dallas and seemed to embrace evangelical leaders who hinted that America was a Christian nation and that Christianity was the only acceptable religion. The president's remarks at the breakfast received wide publicity. Many Jewish leaders who were alienated from the Democratic party because of Louis Farrakhan and the quota issue had second thoughts about supporting the Republican ticket.

Superimposed on all this was the abortion issue. Abortion had been on the political agenda since the Supreme Court's Roe v. Wade decision in 1973. By 1984, it had become a serious problem for the Democratic party. Catholics, a large component of the Democratic coalition, had strongly supported Ronald Reagan in 1980, at least in part because of his outspoken opposition to abortion. By contrast, the Democratic party platform and all its presidential candidates in 1984 strongly supported legal abortion on demand as a woman's right. Not only was the party doing little to recapture Catholic supporters; it seemed to be making it difficult for men and women to be both loyal Democrats and loyal Catholics.

Prominent Catholic Democrats developed a moral rationale to support both their church and their party's platform. They said they were personally opposed to abortion but would not impose their religious views on Americans who disagreed with them. Catholic Democrats taking this line included Governor Mario Cuomo of New York; Senators Edward Kennedy of Massachusetts, Patrick Moynihan of New York, and Patrick Leahy of Vermont; and, before his superiors insisted he leave Congress, Fr. Robert Drinan of Massachusetts.

The Catholic bishops of the United States entered the debate with the so-called seamless garment of life issues which linked opposition to abortion to opposition to nuclear weapons, capital punishment, and other "life" issues. Cardinal Joseph Bernardin of Chicago, popularizer of the idea, called on prolife Catholics to be consistent in their prolife views. The seamless garment notion, which gained wide support from American bishops, was widely interpreted as offering a rationale for antiabortion Catholics to vote for proabortion Democrats who nonetheless held other "prolife" views.

The Catholic bishops were getting accustomed to playing an active and highly visible political role. They had issued their famous pastoral letter on war and peace, a document that seemed to endorse the nuclear freeze movement and had clear overtones of pacifism. The bishops had also announced their intention to write another pastoral letter on the U.S. economy. No one expected it to sing paeans of praise for the free market system.

The nomination of Geraldine Ferraro for vice president was the unpredictable development that made religion the leading campaign issue of 1984. Mrs. Ferraro, a representative of the ethnic Catholics who had been deserting the party, was a strong supporter of abortion rights and expanded abortion funding. Her views on abortion were strongly challenged by Archbishop John O'Connor of New York and indirectly by Archbishop Bernard Law of Boston. Archbishop O'Connor, in turn, was dressed down by Governor Mario Cuomo of New York, but it was obvious that the abortion issue was becoming an even greater political liability for the Democrats.

The Democrats wanted to rehabilitate the "I am personally opposed to abortion but . . ." finesse. Governor Cuomo was chosen to do the job. Cuomo is articulate, emphatic, and interesting. He had delivered an acclaimed keynote address at the Democratic convention. His star was rising for the 1988 presidential nomination. Governor Cuomo's forum was a lecture at the University of Notre Dame sponsored by the university's theology department. He spoke on September 13, 1984, in a speech entitled "Religious Belief and Public Morality: A Catholic Governor's Perspective."

The Notre Dame Law Center invited me to reply and I eagerly did so on September 24. This is the text of my remarks.

SOMEONE HAS REMARKED that this must be an election year: everyone's talking about theology. Suddenly we're hotly debating an issue we thought had been settled at the founding of this nation.

For Catholics the debate has a special interest. We engage in it not only as participants, but, in the minds of some people at least, defendants. Our citizenship is on trial. We are accused of "imposing our views" and "forcing our beliefs" on the community. Our bishops are accused of "violating the constitutional separation of church and state."

These charges have a triple purpose. First, they are designed to create the assumption that the whole question of legal abortion is a "religious" issue. Second, they are designed to create suspicion against Catholics who oppose abortion. But third, and worst of all, they are designed to make Catholics themselves afraid and ashamed to speak out in defense of the unborn. I'm sorry to say that these tactics have been succeeding all too well. Millions of people now take for granted that opposition to abortion can only be grounded in religious dogma; millions assume that Catholics are trying to import an alien doctrine on abortion; and many Catholics are timorously eager to placate potential hostility and bigotry by pleading that although they are "personally opposed" to abortion, they would never "impose their views" on anyone else. At the extreme we have the sort of Catholic politician of whom it's been said that "his religion is so private he won't even impose it on himself."

Today I'd like to begin by discussing some of the major questions that have lately arisen touching the relations between politics and religion. Later I'll conclude with a few words about their meaning for you and me as Catholics.

For I believe that we are now in a time of great testing, a time of arguments down to first principles. Whether the mass media's interest in the church-state debate withers over the next weeks and months, the debate itself will not go away. The questions it raises are too fundamental, and the choices among possible answers too important to the future of the American experiment, for this discussion to be resolved easily or quickly.

Since we are in for a long haul of it, I think it is important at the outset to decide just what it is we are arguing about. That has not been made entirely clear, by antagonists in the arguments and by reporters and commentators, over the past month. At times the discussion has become so obscure that it reminds us of Orwell's observation that "the re-statement of the obvious is the first duty of intelligent men." And, I would add without partisan or ideological intent, of intelligent women. Please, then, permit me to begin by clearing out what seems to me to be some of the underbrush that has grown so luxuriantly around the religion-and-politics debate since the Republican National Convention.

In the first, and hopefully most obvious, place, we are not arguing about the creation of a theocracy, or anything remotely approaching it. While there may be those on one end of the debate who would like to see the United States formally declare itself a "Christian nation"—just as there are those at the other end of the spectrum who would like to see the assumptions and judgments contained in the Humanist Manifestos achieve a constitutional, foundational status in our society—the vast majority of those arguing about the role of religious values in public policy do not want a theocracy in America; do not want one expression of the Judeo-Christian tradition (or any other religious tradition) raised up by government in preference to others; do not want to see religious institutions have a formal role in our political process. Any efforts along these lines would not only threaten the integrity of our political process; they would threaten the integrity of the church.

This last point is worth dwelling on a moment, for it has been largely neglected in the recent debates. These have focused on the integrity of the political process, and not without reason: there have been several occasions where political leaders of both our major parties, in concert with some religious leaders, have given the impression that certain candidates were uniquely favored by God. This is, I think we all would agree, a step over a delicate line. But it is also a problem for the integrity of the church. When the church becomes too immediately identified with any particular partisan organization or agenda, it has lost a measure of its crucial capacity to be a sign of unity in a broken world; to be, as Richard John Neuhaus has put it, a "zone of truth in a world of mendacity." Preserving the integrity of the church should be, conversely, not only a matter of concern for believers, but for all who care about democracy. The churches have played an extremely important role as bridge-builders in our diverse society, and we have every bit as much need of that bridge-building today as in previous generations. A church that becomes identified as the "Democratic party at prayer," a charge laid against some liberal Protestant denominations, as the "Republican party at prayer," a charge laid against some evangelical Protestant denominations, is a church that is risking one of its essential societal roles: that of being ground on which we can gather, not as partisans but as men and women of goodwill, to consider our differences in the context of our common humanity.

So, then, for the sake of our democracy but also for the sake of the church, let us have no hint or trace of theocratic temptations. We are, as our coinage and our Pledge of Allegiance asserts, a nation "under God": that means a nation under God's judgment, constantly reminded by our smallest coin that the true measure of ourselves comes from beyond ourselves. Again, for the church as well as for democracy, let us preserve the integrity of both the political process and the church.

In the second place, we are not arguing about whether "religion and politics should mix." This formula, so simple, is also deceptive and disorienting. Religion, the expression of what theologian Paul Tillich called our "ultimate concern," and politics have "mixed," intermingled, shaped and influenced each other centuries before the conversion of Constantine. And this has been true of our American experiment as well. The claim that American religion has always been "intensely private ... between the individual and God" would surely have come as news to John Winthrop and the Pilgrims, to Jonathan Edwards, to the Abolitionists, to Lincoln, to fifteen generations of the black church, and not least to American Catholics taught by the magisterial John Courtney Murray, architect of the Vatican Council's *Declaration on Religious Liberty*. Throughout our history, religious values have always been a part of the public policy debate. Religious values, particularly the Judeo-Christian tradition's insistence on the inherent dignity and inviolable worth of each individual human life, lie at the root of what Murray called the "American proposition." Yes, other influences shaped the Founders of our republic: Enlightenment modes of political philosophy played their important role, too. But, to borrow a phrase momentarily from the Marxists, "it is no accident" that Benjamin Franklin, one of the deistic Founders, proposed as a device on the Great Seal of the United States a picture of Moses lifting up his staff and dividing the Red Sea while Pharaoh was overwhelmed in its waters, with the motto "rebellion to tyrants is obedience to God." Jefferson, often considered the most implacable foe of "mixing" religion and politics, countered with the suggestion that the Great Seal depict the children of Israel in the wilderness, led by a cloud by day and a pillar of fire by night. From the outset of the American experiment, it was to biblical imagery that the nation most often turned as it sought to understand the full meaning of *novus ordo saeclorum*.

It is often objected that this resort to biblical imagery has resulted in a false religiosity; a kind of hollow piety, symbolized by pre-Super Bowl prayers in the locker room. No doubt there have been Elmer Gantrys in our past, and there will be in our future. But who is more revealing of the essential character of the American proposition? Elmer Gantry? Or Lincoln in his desperate struggle to make sense out of the bloodletting of Civil War: a struggle which, again turning to biblical images and values, yielded the immortal words of the Second Inaugural Address, with both its stark recognition of the sin that had brought immense suffering and its ennobling call to charity among both victors and vanquished?

Religion and politics have thus always "mixed" in America, if what we are talking about is religious values and public policy. What the Founders wisely understood was that religious *institutions* should not become unnecessarily entangled with the political process. From this understanding arose the twin principles of the First Amendment: no established church, and no state coercion over religious belief and practice, within the limits of maintaining the public order. These principles, viewed skeptically for so long by a universal church more accustomed to European usages, came to be enshrined in the Second Vatican Council's *Declaration on Religious Liberty*, which was, in no small measure, the gift of American Catholicism to the church throughout the world.

The Constitutional separation of church and state is thus a question of institutional distinctiveness and integrity. It was never intended to rule religiously based values out of order in the public arena. Yet that is precisely what some among us would do: disqualify an argument or a public policy from constitutional consideration if its roots are "religious."

This brings us to the third misconception of the church-state debate.

The great bulk of commentary in recent weeks has been to the effect that the new church-state debate was caused by the rise of the religious new right, and its allies in the Catholic hierarchy. This is too simple an analysis, and fails to take the measure of a longer-standing phenomenon on our national life: the rise of a militant secular-separationist perspective on the constitutional questions that seek to rule religiously based values "out of order" in the public arena. Let us be precise about the agenda being pursued here. The issue was not tuition tax credits. The issue was much more fundamental: the issue was whether any values that were explicitly religious in origin would be admitted to public consideration in the conduct of the public's business. The "wall of separation," according to these activists, sundered not only religious *institutions* and the institutions of the state; it stood fast between religiously based *values* and the debate over the public business. Any appeal to a religiously based value to buttress an argument for this or that public policy option was thus a "violation of the separation of church and state."

However, the application of this secular principle has been schizophrenic to say the least. The clergy were revered when they marched at Selma, joined antiwar sit-ins and helped boycott lettuce—they are reviled when they speak out against abortion. Anyone who studies these subjects soon gets familiar with the double standard.

The secular-separationist wave had to crest eventually, though; since the overwhelming majority of the American people ground their public faith and lives in religiously based values, a collision was inevitable. We are now living in the noise and confusion of that collision. The religious new right, composed largely of evangelical Protestants pushed to the margins of our culture and our politics since the days of the Scopes trial, kicked a tripwire reminding us that there could not be a permanent chasm between the values allowed in to the public arena, and the religiously based values of the American people.

The coalition that has formed between these evangelicals (who represent, from some estimates, as many as 60 million Americans) and Roman Catholics is both unprecedented and somewhat surprising. I think at least two important reasons explain some of this new coalition activity. First, there have been significant changes within the evangelical community, both in terms of its own self-understanding and in its understanding of its relationship to Catholicism. It is no longer possible to equate the words "evangelical" and "fundamentalist," for example. Many evangelicals are fundamentalists in their approach to Scripture, of course; but others are not. Some evangelicals harbor anti-Catholic bias; most do not. Anti-Catholicism is perhaps more, and certainly no less, predictable in certain cultural quarters of the secular-separationist world than it is among evangelicals. Most importantly, evangelicals saw themselves as coming in from the cultural and political wilderness, a process not unlike that of Catholic ethnics. They looked and saw an America deeply troubled by drugs, pornography, and abortion and determined to do something about it. From altered self-understanding came the possibility of altered ecumenical relations.

In addition to these momentous changes, Catholics began to react against the secular-separationist agenda. Catholics saw the confusion on the Supreme Court, which would allow state funds for books in parish schools but not for "instructional materials" such as maps. Catholics saw the crude caricatures involved in the use of stereotyped priests and nuns for advertisements, didn't find much funny in "Saturday Night Live's" Father Guido Sarducci, and wondered what was going on in the minds that could produce such images. But most importantly, Catholics experienced the hypocrisy of the abortion debate. They saw an issue of the utmost importance to constitutional first principles—who shall be within the boundaries of our community's sense of obligation and protection?—dismissed as a "Catholic issue," an unconstitutional "mixing of religion and politics." We were accused of "trying to impose our religious values on others." One can only absorb so much of this falsification, and then one reacts.

The principled resistance to "imposing one's religious views" on a pluralistic society is a favorite ploy of the "I'm personally opposed to abortion but . . ." school of politician. Their dilemma is that they want to retain their Catholic credentials but realize that in today's Democratic party to be upwardly mobile is to be very liberal and to be very liberal is to be a feminist and to be a feminist is to be for abortion. I won't quarrel with their political game plan, but their rationale is absurd.

First of all, abortion is not a Catholic issue, nor a Mormon issue, nor a Lutheran issue. It is an ethical issue that the Supreme Court (the same Court that opened the floodgates in 1973) has specifically found is "as much a reflection of traditionalist values toward abortion, as it is an embodiment of the view of any particular religion." The Court also found in its decision of June 30, 1980, in *Harris v. McRae* that "it does not follow that a statute violates the Establishment Clause because it happens to coincide or harmonize with the tenets of some or all religions. That the Judeo-Christian religions opposed stealing does not mean that a . . . government may not, consistent with the Establishment Clause, enact laws prohibiting larceny."

In support of their spurious argument spurious analogies are necessary such as identifying abortion, which by definition and intention involves the destruction of innocent human life, with the issues of birth control or divorce, which do not.

The distinctions are of transcendent importance because we're talking about a basic human right, the first civil right, enshrined in our nation's birth certificate where we are reminded that all men are created equal and are endowed by their Creator with certain inalienable rights—the first of which is life. Is the protection of this human right an impermissible religious intrusion?

Another way of expressing one's reluctance to impose one's values on a society is to require a consensus before supporting any changes in the law. You will note that this is a highly selective requirement applying only to abortion legislation. No consensus was demanded before adopting the Civil Rights Act of 1964 or Fair Housing legislation—these were right and their proponents helped *create* a consensus by advocacy and example and by understanding that the law itself can be an excellent teacher. No, when the cause was the abolition of slavery or the codification of civil rights, the moral thing to do was to push for the changes and to help achieve the consensus which followed.

The whole notion of morality by consensus is a curious one. I've often thought that if Jesus had taken a poll he would never have preached the gospel.

And so to argue, then, that the religious new right has "caused" this new church-state debate is to claim both too much and too little. Had the religiously based values of the great majority of the American people not been systematically ruled out of order in public discourse over the past twenty years, there would have been no tripwire in the national consciousness to be kicked. Had Catholics not, concurrently, seen a matter of great importance to them categorically ghettoized as a "Catholic issue," and thus an issue that ought not be treated in the public arena, there would have been no coalition between evangelicals and Catholics. That coalition may not last forever: but for the moment, it has been of sufficient weight to have forced to the surface of our public debate a set of arguments that has been going on, as a kind of subterranean civil war of cultures, for at least a generation.

The combination of passion and ignorance can be deadly, and so let us remind ourselves that we ought to argue these matters seriously without taking ourselves with ultimate seriousness; it suggests that we ought to make clear our opinions. May I do so briefly, bringing matters down from the theoretical to the practical: what should we do to facilitate a debate on religious values and public policy that strengthens the integrity of the church and the political process?

I would suggest in the first place that we insist on rigorous intellectual consistency in these arguments. Not a few observers have noted that many of the same voices who hailed the American bishops as "prophetic" when they tacitly endorsed the nuclear freeze now find the bishops "scary" when the issue turns to abortion. This is hypocrisy. The bishops have the clear right (and, in Catholic theory, responsibility) to make clear what they think are the appropriate moral criteria for forming and shaping public policy, on issues ranging from national security to domestic welfare policy to abortion. If the bishops enter the public arena to propound these criteria, they have an obligation to do so in language and imagery that is accessible to a pluralistic audience, and not just to Catholics. In our democracy, the bishops clearly have the right to go farther and to suggest what in their prudential judgments the public policies most likely to meet the test of their moral criteria would be. In Catholic theory, the bishops' prudential judgment is to be weighed seriously and respectfully; it is not weighted with the same gravity, however, as the bishops' teaching about the normative moral framework that should guide public policy.

Thus, the Catholic theory about the teaching role of religious leadership. Such a model would seem appropriate for religious leaders of other denominations in a pluralistic democracy such as our own. This model protects the constitutional right of the bishops as citizens to speak their minds about the public business; it also protects the integrity of the political process from unwarranted entanglements with religious institutions. Yet this model, which would seem to be the essence of reasonableness in a liberal, democratic society, is now under attack. At least one nationally syndicated columnist has suggested that the bishops had better mind their manners on the subject of abortion or the tax-exempt status of church property could be jeopardized: the threat of a bully, not of a man of justice, to recall Thomas More's reproach to Cromwell in *A Man for All Seasons*.

Here the question of consistency comes clear. Had the archbishop of New York quizzed a conservative Catholic president about his commitment to nuclear arms control, would there have been impassioned hand-wringing at the *New York Times* editorial board about "mixing politics and religion"? Yet this is precisely what happened when the archbishop of New York questioned a liberal Democratic candidate for vice president about her approach to the public policy of abortion. Why is it that Archbishop O'Connor threatens the separation of church and state when he tries to clarify Catholic teaching about abortion, and the Reverend Jesse Jackson doesn't when he organizes a partisan political campaign through the agency of dozens of churches? These confusions are not merely a matter of anti-Catholic bias, although that is undoubtedly present; they reflect the chaotic condition of public understanding on the larger questions of religious values and the public policy debate.

I cannot think of a clearer illustration of this double standard than by quoting from a letter sent to Archbishop John R. Roach, then President of the National Conference of Catholic Bishops. This letter appeared in the New York diocesan newspaper, *Catholic New York,* on July 7, 1983:

> As an American and a Catholic I am proud of you. It would have been easy to compromise your position so as to offend no one. You chose instead to tend to your duties as shepherds, to teach the moral law as best you can. You can do no more. Our church has sometimes been accused of not having spoken out when it might have. Now you, our Bishops, show the courage and moral judgment to meet this issue of nuclear holocaust with a collective expression of where the church in America stands.

This letter was signed by the present governor of New York, Mario Cuomo.

Churches as institutions should not play a formal role in our political process, both for the sake of their own integrity as well as the integrity of our politics. Church leaders, on the other hand, have every right to make publicly clear their views on both specific issues and, more importantly, on the moral norms that should guide our approach to those issues. If religious leaders are ruled constitutionally out of bounds in these debates because they make explicit reference to the religious bases of the values they see as normative, then an unconstitutional, illiberal act of bigotry has taken place. And what does this say about our devotion to pluralism?

Moreover, all religious leaders should be held to the same standard (i.e. not institutional entanglement, but full play for the appeal to religiously based values in arguing public business). Black and white, Protestant, Jewish, and Catholic: all should observe the same limits. The obverse of this delimitation of roles is that public officials must take all possible precautions to avoid even the appearance of giving the state's favor to one expression of the Judeo-Christian traditions over others. In my view, there is nothing unconstitutional or inappropriate in a president making clear his or her understanding that religiously based values have had, and will continue to have, a crucial, formative role in our democratic experiment. If Washington, Lincoln, and Roosevelt could do so, why not Ronald Reagan? The bounds of sensitivity are crossed, however, if and when a president seems to give public favor to one denomination or sect over others. No more than any other citizen can we expect a president to put his conscience into the closet during his or her term of office. We can expect that all presidents will hold to the distinction between religious institutions and religious values in framing their approach to these questions.

Consistency is one antidote to hypocrisy. So, too, is a theory and practice of pluralism that meets the twin tests of constitutional integrity and religious liberty. All of us have heard it said recently that the new church-state debate is a threat to American "pluralism." That it could be, were it a debate about the establishment of a theocracy. But since it is not, it is worth observing that the contemporary nervousness over threats to "pluralism" has the issue precisely backwards. According to the secular-separationist orthodoxy, so often reflected in the national media, it is the overt appeal to religiously based values in the public arena that threatens pluralism. In fact, it is much more likely that it is precisely the democracy's commitment to religious liberty, including the freedom not to believe. Our democratic experiment's commitment to pluralism is not sustained today by abstract allegiance to the Enlightenment; it is sustained by fundamental themes in the Judeo-Christian tradition, particularly that tradition's insistence on the inviolability of individual conscience. To drive religiously based values out of the public arena is the real threat to pluralism. A commitment to pluralism, like any other significant commitment, must be sustained by a frame of reference that transcends the here and now; or as Chesterton put it, "An open mind, like an open mouth, should close on something."

For a public arena shorn of the religiously based values of the American people would not remain empty for long. The values vacuum is filled by the raw pursuit of interests, and politics deteriorates into the mere quest for power in its most base form: the capacity to thwart others. The church-state debate upon which we are now engaged is, from one angle of vision, a debate over whether a "civil war by other means" (as Alasdair MacIntyre has put it) will break out with real ferocity, or whether it can be healed through the creation of a new public philosophy, able to provide moral coordinates for the conduct of the American experiment in ways that can be followed by both religious believers and their nonbelieving fellow citizens.

American Catholics are in a privileged position to make

enormously useful contributions to the development of such a public philosophy. We are the inheritors of a two-thousand-year-old tradition of careful thought about the relationship between personal conscience and public policy. We do not come to the complexities of these issues as biblical literalists, or as philosophical naifs; and our natural law tradition provides a means for mediating religious values into the public arena in a publicly accessible way. The bedrock principles of Catholic social ethics—personalism, pluralism, and the common good—are all notions eminently suitable for incorporation into a revivified public philosophy in America. The Catholic principle of subsidiarity is also relevant to today's political culture, and holds out the prospect of being one of those bridge-concepts that sets common ground between ideologically divided foes. Catholics know, in their ethnic bones, the truth of Walter Lippman's observations that "Liberty is not the natural state of man, but the achievement of an organized society." No institution in the Western world has more experience with the tough questions of societal organization than the Roman Catholic Church; no institution in America has benefited more from the conduct of the American experiment than American Catholicism. Might I suggest that it is time for American Catholics, particularly Catholic intellectuals, writers, and public officials, to begin making a distinctively Catholic contribution to this preeminent task of reconstituting an effective public philosophy capable of sustaining the future of the American proposition? Might I also suggest that considerably more material will be found for such a task in the writings of John Courtney Murray than in a dozen volumes extolling "Marxist analysis"?

All government is compulsion unless the whole nation unanimously agrees on a given proposition. Absent this (and it's nearly always absent) some people's views will be imposed on others. Our ideal has been to minimize the compulsion and to utilize persuasion. But this requires, as Joseph Sobran calls it, "an ethos of fair and civil discussion." It is a sad fact that too many liberals, normally eloquent champions of free speech, by misrepresenting the nature of this issue and the goals of the prolife movement, have eroded that ethos. They have literally told us to go sit in the back of the bus.

The role of Catholic public officials in the important task of revitalizing American politics through the free market of religious competition intended by our Founding Fathers deserves some brief reflection.

The Catholic public official, like his Catholic fellow citizens, ought not come to this discussion under a cloud of suspicion. It is well to think back to the example of John F. Kennedy before the Greater Houston Ministerial Association; but the terms of the fundamental debate have shifted dramatically since 1960. The question today is not whether a Roman Catholic commitment is compatible with American public office; the question is whether the American experiment can survive the sterilization of the public arena that takes place when religiously based values are systematically ruled out of order in the public discourse.

It is ironically the same Catholics who were once suspect on the grounds of their discomfort with pluralism who now have an opportunity to help reconstitute an American pluralism in which there is space for religiously based values in the public arena. As Catholic public officials, we do not come to the public debate on church-state matters with a scarlet "C" sewn to our breast.

The National Conference of Catholic Bishops, in its recent statement on the church-state debate, correctly noted that a Catholic public official cannot finally sunder personal conscience and civic responsibility. Most of us would, I hope, subscribe to that teaching. The discussion gets more interesting, and more diffficult, when we try to define with precision just what the positive responsibilities of the Catholic public official are, particularly when he or she is called upon to enforce a law with which they are in conscientious disagreement, be that a capital punishment statute or the abortion liberty as defined by the Supreme Court in *Roe v. Wade* and subsequent rulings.

Since the abortion issue is so often the centerpiece of these arguments, let me address that briefly.

It is clearly insufficient for a Catholic public official to hold that his or her personal, conscientious objection to abortion as a matter of personal choice for himself or herself ends the matter. As Stephen Chapman says, it doesn't make sense to say an abortion takes a life *and* it should be allowed. If a fetus represents a human life, its disposition cannot be strictly a private matter. It is just as clear that Catholic public officials must abide by their oath of office to enforce the laws. But what else ought we to do?

First, we ought to make use of the educative potential of public office to make clear that abortion is not, at bottom, a "Catholic issue," but rather a moral and civil rights issue, a humanitarian issue, and a constitutional issue of the first importance. The abortion liberty, we should insist, is a profoundly narrow-minded, illiberal position; it constricts, rather than expands, the scope of liberty properly understood. It draws in, rather than expands, the community of the protected. These are, or ought to be, issues of concern far beyond the American Catholic community. Our approach to the problem of profligate abortion must be couched in terms like these, publicly accessible and understandable terms.

Second, we ought to do everything in our power to make abortion a less-immediate resort for the bearer of an unwanted child. This will involve, as others have suggested, government support for adoption services and for health care during pregnancy, to cite but two examples of positive governmental intervention into this problem. But it should also involve serious and careful reconsideration of a welfare system that currently rewards pregnancies out of wedlock, and that has contributed to the erosion of the family structure among the poor. The Catholic commitment to a social ethics in which consequences (not merely intentions) carry moral weight suggests that we examine our public conscience on the ways by which we have tried to meet the needs of the weakest among us, and ask whether or not these efforts have not in some circumstances actually contributed to the problems they were intended to solve.

Those who point out that solving the abortion issue through constitutional or legal action involves prudential judgments on which Catholics may in good conscience disagree are correct in their basic assertion. They may even be correct in their claim that there is no effective public consensus at present capable of sustaining a constitutional prohibition of abortion. But the status quo need not remain forever, and we cannot in conscience be satisfied with a status quo in which one and a half million children are killed every year, no matter how sympathetic we may be to the personal tragedies involved when parents take the decision to abort their offspring. The duty of one who regards abortion as wrong is not to bemoan the absence of a consensus against abortion, but to help lead the effort to achieve one. Catholic public officials have, in my judgment, a moral and civic obligation to clarify precisely what is at stake in the abortion controversy (and not only for the unborn child, but for the moral and political health of the American experiment); we have a moral and civic obligation to help disentangle this fundamental question of constitutional protection from the confusing sound of rhetoric involved when "separation of church and state" and feminist ideology are brought into the debate; and we have a moral and civic obligation to create structures in society that make the first resort to abortion in the case of unwanted pregnancy less likely. Ultimately, as Professor John Noonan has said so eloquently, the abortion liberty must be overcome "in love." But between now and then, there is much we can do in addition to declaring the state of our personal consciences.

It has been said here recently that Catholics in their own belief and behavior don't differ significantly from the rest of the population on the issue of legal abortion. I hope that isn't quite true. But there is at least some truth in it, as all of us must admit.

And yet there is another side of this fact: it means that the prolife movement itself is no more Catholic than non-Catholic. It gives the lie to the charge that we are trying to impose a uniquely Catholic position.

When the great wave of Catholic immigration to America occurred in the nineteenth century, Catholics didn't import prolife attitudes. These were already here. The several states had passed their own laws restricting and prohibiting abortion, for reasons that had nothing to do with Catholic teaching.

This was the consensus, not only of the United States, but of all civilized people. *Abortion was wrong.* The Supreme Court didn't express a new consensus in 1973; it attacked the consensus that already existed, by striking down not only the most restrictive but *even the most liberal* abortion laws then in existence. It informed the legislatures of all fifty states that they were all, in diverse ways, violating the Constitution. None of those legislatures, Republican or Democrat, conservative or liberal, had ever understood the Constitution properly. The consensus was wrong, even at its permissive margin. So said the Court.

The Catholic Church has introduced nothing foreign or novel. It has merely been the most important institution to insist on the moral consensus the Court assaulted. It has spoken in harmony with many non-Catholics.

Samuel Johnson once observed, "Mankind more frequently requires to be reminded than informed." That is all we are doing: at a time when the moral consensus of the West is under assault, we are reminding this nation of its traditional membership in that consensus. That is what moral authority is for: not to introduce doctrinal novelties, not to compete for power with those who currently hold power, but to remind the powerful of the moral limits of power. True authority is not a rival but a moral yardstick of power.

I am not referring here to the teaching authority of the

Church as such: I'm talking about the authority of moral law in the experience of all mankind, the moral law written in our hearts, the moral law without which it is nonsense to speak of "rights."

Catholics neither have nor claim any monopoly of that law. We do have a duty to maintain it, and to be willing to stand up to speak for it when the state violates it. This is a duty wholly distinct from our duty to propagate our faith. The gospel is the good news; but the moral law is not news at all, it is what we know in our hearts already.

The abortion issue is at once the hardest and the most typical case involved in the whole complex area of religiously based values and public policy. It is the hardest case because of the depth of feelings involved on all sides, and because of the fantastic obfuscation that has grown around the issue since *Roe v. Wade*. It is the most typical case because the furor surrounding it illustrates graphically the condition of a public arena deliberately shorn of religiously based values; we have lost the ability to conduct moral arguments in the public arena, because we have no agreement on the coordinates that should guide and shape such debate. This means that the abortion issue cannot be resolved under the conditions of what Richard Neuhaus has called the "Naked Public Square." Until we reestablish the legitimacy of an appeal to religiously based values in the conduct of the public debate over the public business, the abortion debate will remain a case of barely-restrained "civil war carried on by other means." Thus our essential difficulty, and the debate surrounding it, are not the result of a new intervention by the Catholic hierarchy into the political affairs of the nation. The truth may be precisely the opposite; that the bishops' entry, coupled with the rise of evangelical Protestantism, has brought about a critical mass of dissatisfaction with the secular-separationist perspective in its commitment to the maintenance of a public square uncontaminated by religious values. Turning that dissatisfaction into the positive reconstruction of a public philosophy capable of sustaining the American experiment into its third century is a noble task to which all of us are called.

Especially called are you, the students of Notre Dame. Father Theodore Hesburgh, in an address to the faculty in January 1982, said:

> Obviously, we are swimming against the current when we profess the eternal and the spiritual to an age completely caught up in temporal and material concerns. It is not easy to engage in intellectual inquiry in the context of the Christian message in a world that often rejects the Good News. How to teach students to cherish values, prayer, grace and eternal life when they are surrounded by a sea of vice, unbelief, cynicism, and anomie, all dressed up to look sophisticated and modern, something they mostly aspire to be. . . .
>
> Moral relativism gives us a society that is only relatively moral and we are sick of that, very sick indeed.

Nearly two weeks ago on this campus the governor proposed a hypothetical case:

> Put aside what God expects—assume if you like there is no God—then the greatest thing still left to us is life.

That remark misses a point of terrifying importance, a point that was made by Professor Paul Eidelberg:

> Unless there is a Being superior than man, nothing in theory prevents some men from degrading other men to the level of subhuman.

The age of Dachau and Auschwitz and the Gulag verify Eidelberg's insight. How many times must we learn that, when moral values are excluded from the public square, raw force alone settles the issue?

I have always believed that the purpose of a Christian education is to help us *change the world.* I have never heard a commencement address admonish graduates to "go out there and *don't* change the world"!

No matter what the failings and fears of our fellow Catholics, no matter how far short we ourselves may fall at times, we have the duty to speak out. To fail to speak, to bear witness to our commitment, is not the virtue of prudence: it is self-serving expediency.

We need not wait for our bishops to speak out. We can and must do it ourselves. The most helpless members of our society need us. Don't fail them! Don't be afraid to speak! Don't let anyone make you ashamed to stand up as a Catholic for all human beings! Loving people who can't love you back is no small thing! And after you have encountered all the ambiguities, syllogisms, and sophistries, and after the last hair has been split, don't let them make you ashamed to be a Catholic!

And forgive some unsolicited advice, but you will find it awfully hard to go anywhere in the world without your soul tagging along. And you needn't be too deferential if someone tells you a preborn baby's life is too trivial to protect. You might remember that, while this is the age of abortion, it also is the age of Dachau and Auschwitz and the Gulag.

St. Ambrose said, "Not only for every idle word must man render an account, but for every idle silence."

Charles Peguy has said, "If you possess the truth and remain silent you become the accomplice of liars and forgers."

Elie Wiesel, who survived Auschwitz, has said, "Apathy towards evil is man's greatest sin."

And so—do you change the world or does the world change you?

A man sent me a letter some time ago that he had received from perhaps the most famous of our senators—the senator's letter is dated August 3, 1971. It contains the following language:

While the deep concern of a woman bearing an unwanted child merits consideration and sympathy, it is my personal feeling that the legalization of abortion on demand is not in accordance with the values which our civilization places on human life. Wanted or unwanted, I believe that human life, even at its earliest stages, has certain rights which must be recognized—the right to be born, the right to love, the right to grow old.

When history looks back to this era it should recognize this generation as one which cared about human beings enough to halt the practice of war, to provide a decent living for every family, and to fulfill its responsibility to its children from the very moment of conception.

A beautiful statement—in 1971. But today that senator, a prominent Catholic, does not support our legislation and hasn't for the ten years I've been in Congress. He's repeatedly voted to use tax funds to pay for abortions, and yet if he would assume the leadership of our movement we would prevail. Believe me, one person can move mountains.

The day before he was assassinated in 1968, Dr. Martin Luther King, Jr., reflected out loud with an audience about the times in which he lived. And he said, "If I were standing at the beginning of time, with the possibility of a general and panoramic view of the whole of human history up to now, and the Almighty said to me, 'Martin Luther King, which age would you like to live in?' . . . I would turn to the Almighty and say, 'If you would allow me to live just a few years in the second half of the Twentieth Century, I will be happy.' Now that's a strange statement to make because the world is all messed up. But I know, somehow, that only when it is dark enough, can you see the stars."

And so I ask again, do you change the world or does the world change you?

There was a "Just Man" many centuries ago who tried to save Sodom from destruction. Ignoring his warning, mocking him with silence, the inhabitants shielded themselves with indifference. But still he persisted, and taking pity on him, a child asked, "Why do you go on?" The Just Man replied that in the beginning, he thought he could change man. "Today," he said, "I know I cannot. If I still shout and scream it's to prevent them from changing me!"

I hope you go out and change the world!

THREE

Religion and the Constitution: A Debate

The First Amendment to the Constitution reads, in part: "Congress shall make no law respecting an establishment of religion or prohibiting the free exercise thereof." Many current church-state controversies are battles over the meaning of this sentence. These include the constitutional and political struggles over school prayer, equal access, tuition tax credits, the creationism-evolution issue, and public display of religious symbols. The fact is that the First Amendment's words about religion are not entirely clear. Does the First Amendment build a wall of separation between church and state? How can a nation that is largely populated by religious believers be strictly neutral in matters of religion? If government is to permit free exercise of religion, how are the rights of nonbelievers to be guaranteed?

These questions were aired in 1984 at a forum on Religion and the Constitution sponsored by the American Enterprise Institute. I participated in a debate-discussion with Walter Berns of the AEI, Edd Doerr of Americans for Religious Liberty, and Barry Lynn of the American Civil Liberties Union. It was a vigorous debate and an illuminating discussion, as you will see for yourself.

JOHN CHARLES DALY, former ABC News chief: This public policy forum, one of a series presented by the American

Enterprise Institute, examines the relationship of church and state under the Constitution of the United States. Our subject: religion and the Constitution.

Our Constitution, hammered out in the long debate in Philadelphia in 1787, went to the states for ratification bearing one reference to religion. Article VI states: "No religious Test shall ever be required as a Qualification to any Office or public Trust under the United States."

After months of debate in the states, the Constitution was ratified. The states made it clear, however, that the First Congress was expected to act immediately on amendments protecting specific rights, among them religious rights. In its first sitting then, the Congress debated and passed, and the states subsequently ratified, ten amendments—our Bill of Rights.

The First Amendment declares, in part: "Congress shall make no law respecting an establishment of religion"—this is known as the Establishment Clause—"or prohibiting the free exercise thereof"—this is known as the Free Exercise Clause.

This brief, albeit comprehensive, declaration of religious rights was distilled from a familiar background. The thirteen colonies were settled substantially by families fleeing religious persecution in England and elsewhere in Europe, and religion was a dominant factor in the colonies where, by the way, religious persecution was not entirely unknown.

At the time of our Revolution, nine of the thirteen colonies still had established religions—the Puritan Congregational church in Massachusetts, New Hampshire, and Connecticut, and the Anglican church in New York, Maryland, Virginia, North and South Carolina, and Georgia. Moreover, five states had established religions as the First Amendment was drafted, and restrictions of one kind or another affecting some religious beliefs existed in five other states.

The two clauses, the Establishment Clause and the Free Exercise Clause, have been intensely debated as to their scope and meaning and the original intent of the founders concerning them. In modern times, that intensity of debate increased markedly in 1947, with the Supreme Court decision in *Everson v. Board of Education*. In its opinion the Court held that the Establishment Clause was made wholly applicable to the states by the Fourteenth Amendment's Due Process Clause, and over time the application of both the Establishment and the Free Exercise clauses to the states through the Fourteenth Amendment played a major role in other cases before the Supreme Court. There were cases involving Sunday closing laws and the right to unemployment benefits when a religiously mandated Saturday non-workday made many jobs unavailable. In Wisconsin, there was the refusal on religious grounds by members of the Old Order Amish to send their children to school past the eighth grade; in Maryland, a commission was denied to a notary public because the candidate would not declare a belief in God; in Tennessee, a law prohibited ministers from serving in the legislature or serving as delegates to the Constitutional Convention; all were issues that came before the Court.

In very recent times, on the legislative front, proposed amendments have been defeated in the Senate concerning voluntary vocal and silent prayer. The Congress rejected and then passed an "equal access" bill, designed to ensure that student religious groups in public high schools have the same rights as secular student clubs to meet on school grounds. Church groups, by the way, were divided on that bill, and civil liberties experts, who normally agree on almost all sensitive legislation of this kind, also were in disagreement.

There are other issues that seem pressing to various constituencies: teaching creationism in science education; the Supreme Court's recent creche decision, affirming the constitutionality of including religious symbols in holiday displays on public ground; and issues such as conscientious objector status in military registration, and the naming of an official ambassador to the Vatican.

To guide us through this complex and contentious relationship between the Constitution and religion, we have an expert panel. Mr. Walter Berns is John M. Olin Distinguished Scholar in Constitutional and Legal Studies at the American Enterprise Institute and the author of *The First Amendment and the Future of American Democracy*. Representative Henry J. Hyde, Republican member of the House of Representatives from Illinois, is serving his fifth term. Representative Hyde is a member of the House Judiciary Committee and serves on the Subcommittee on Courts, Civil Liberties, and the Administration of Justice. Mr. Edd Doerr is executive director of Americans for Religious Liberty, and former editor of *Church and State* magazine. And the Reverend Barry Lynn is legislative counsel in the Washington office of the American Civil Liberties Union. He has been legislative counsel in the Office for Church in Society, United Church of Christ and is also an ordained minister of the United Church of Christ.

To begin, gentlemen, I would pose the same question to each of you in turn. Does government have an obligation to support religion as one way of helping to sustain a free society? Our nation's motto is "In God We Trust." The president, members of Congress, judges, and other public servants often swear their oaths of office on the Bible. Each day of the congressional session begins with the prayer for guidance. Should government help strengthen religious values in other ways?

HENRY J. HYDE, U.S. representative (Republican, Illinois): I think government may do so within the confines of the Constitution, as long as it does not prefer one sect or religious group over another. The hostility toward all religion that seems to be the result of the *Everson* case was never before true. We have had government support for chaplains, not only in the military, but in the House and Senate, and James Madison was on the committee that provided for them. We always have had relationships of a sort between religious groups and government, but the Constitution requires that they be such as not to set up a state religion, a national religion, and, certainly, not to prefer one religion over another.

EDD DOERR, executive director, Americans for Religious Liberty: The best thing that the state can do for religion is to keep its hands off it, to let religion stay in the private sector. Government should not force citizens involuntarily, through taxation, to support religion. Government should not meddle with the religious lives of children or adults. It should not discriminate in any way for or against various churches. Unfortunately, though our history for two centuries since the adoption of the Constitution has been one of reaffirming and furthering the separation of church and state that Jefferson and Madison spoke so highly of, in the last few years we have seen tremendous efforts toward the piecemeal repeal of the First Amendment. There are efforts in state capitals and in Congress to tax people for the support of religious institutions, efforts to amend the Constitution to authorize civil servants to meddle with children's religious lives, and efforts by government to interfere with the conscience rights of women to determine whether or not they will become mothers. The president recently extended diplomatic relations to a single church to the exclusion of all others. These are some of the examples of how government has been moving away from the neutrality toward religion that is required by the Constitution.

WALTER BERNS, John M. Olin Distinguished Scholar in Constitutional and Legal Studies, American Enterprise Institute: Mr. Daly, in your question you used the word "obligation," that is, does the government have an obligation to support religious values? Strictly speaking, of course, the government has no obligation in the sense that it has a constitutional obligation, as stated in Article IV of the Constitution, to guarantee a republican form of government to each of the states. So the question really is not whether the government has an obligation, but whether it would be well advised to support religion, or whether there are some compelling reasons why it should. I agree with Mr. Doerr that, of course, the purpose of the First Amendment is to subordinate religion to the private sphere. The question then becomes whether the government is *forbidden* by the First Amendment to provide assistance to religion in the private sphere and to act in one way or another to see to it that religion in the private sphere maintains its vitality. The answer to that question probably turns on whether it is understood by us, as it was understood by Americans in the beginning, that there is some connection between the sort of moral training that the churches provide and a healthy, liberal democracy in the United States. That, I think, is the way the issue should be phrased.

BARRY W. LYNN, legislative counsel, American Civil Liberties Union: It is important that we recognize not only that the government may not be hostile to religion, but that it must be very strictly neutral regarding religion. This means at least several things. First, it means the government must preserve the right of conscience for all Americans, so that persons are not forced to support religious practices with which they disagree. Second, it means that the government must scrupulously avoid involvement in religious matters and may not supervise religious institutions. Third, neutrality means the government must not create political warfare over sectarian religious matters. And, finally, government neutrality regarding religion is necessary so as not to degrade the practice of religion itself.

The question for this decade and the decades to come is not so much what the framers may have thought about the Constitution nearly 200 years ago, but how those majestic generalities in the First Amendment are to be construed today as concrete restraints on what the government can do.

MR. BERNS: In other words, the Constitution changes its meaning over time?

MR. LYNN: I think the Constitution is a living document; it must remain such. In fact, it is very interesting that Mr. Hyde mentioned that James Madison voted for the establishment of congressional chaplains. It is important to mention that several years later as president, he wrote a document opposing the continuation of the practice of having congressional chaplains because he felt it was a First Amendment violation. Even if not at the beginning, by the time he was president I am sure he would have fit very well in the American Civil Liberties Union.

MR. BERNS: Yes, but the issue is whether the Constitution changes its meaning over time and, apparently, your answer to that is, "Yes, indeed, it does change its meaning over time." So what controls the direction in which the constitution moves?

MR. LYNN: The way in which, and the circumstances under which, one delicately balances the requirements of the Free Exercise Clause with the guarantee that there shall be no establishment of religion. There is a tension between the religion clauses, whether or not the framers of the Constitution initially recognized it. To call it a tension is perhaps too polite. In some ways there is a contradiction between those two clauses, and to the maximum extent possible, we must guarantee the right of conscience and the right of free exercise, so that persons may exercise their consciences in complete accord with their religious beliefs.

REPRESENTATIVE HYDE: I agree with everything you have said, Mr. Lynn, but much more important and fundamental is the question Mr. Berns raised: How does this "living" document change, and how do people on the bench of the Supreme Court, through some insight—or, as Justice Jackson said in his concurring opinion in *Everson*, through "no law but our own prepossession"—determine what this document means today, rather than leaving this determination to the legislative branch, which is accountable, electable, and recallable by the people? It seems to me that we have gotten away from the consent of the governed and are back to the divine right of kings.

MR. LYNN: By creating this dichotomy, one creates the possibility that majority rule, as reflected by members of Congress and their constituents, will be the arbiter, the final arbiter, of constitutional values. It has been clear since *Marbury v. Madison* that in fact it is the Supreme Court that is the arbiter, finally of what the First Amendment and the rest of the Constitution means, and that is the way it should be.

REPRESENTATIVE HYDE: Yes, but I would suggest that the task of the court is to adjudicate, and not to legislate, not to find things in the Constitution that are not there, that never were contemplated by the framers. The framers, in their wisdom, provided a way to amend the Constitution, but they made it tough. They required an extraordinary majority in the House and in the Senate for passage of an amendment, and thirty-eight states to ratify. That is tough. But they did not say that a majority of five men or women on the court can change the Constitution. They said, "Go out to the people and change it." That is what we have gotten away from.

MR. DOERR: Whether the Court changes the Constitution is a matter of opinion, but the Constitution was written 200 years ago, and the founders are long since dead. When there is an apparent conflict over constitutional rights, the Supreme Court does not exactly legislate, but it settles disputes between parties, between those who go into court with a real controversy. Both parties make constitutional claims, and the Supreme Court and the lower federal courts have to decide who has the better claim.

It is stretching things to say that the Court is legislating.

The justices are the guardians of the Constitution, and without them, Congress could run roughshod over our liberties, as it has sometimes done in the heat of passion.

MR. BERNS: The question is, Are they guardians of a Constitution that has a relatively fixed meaning, or are they guardians of something that they themselves create? If they are the guardians of something that they themselves create, there is no problem here at all, because they will guard it as a father guards his child, and the miser his money.

MR. DOERR: What is your solution to that?

MR. BERNS: Solution to what? I just keep asking whether the Constitution changes its meaning; perhaps we have to settle that before we go any further.

MR. LYNN: It is also important to realize that most of what was in the minds of the people in the Congress that sent the Bill of Rights out to the states and certainly most of what was in the minds of the state legislators who ratified the Bill of Rights is totally unknown information. It is not possible for us to go back and seek the original intention.

MR. BERNS: That is not so. We know what went on in the Congress. We know what James Madison said in the First Congress in 1789. We know what Samuel Livermore said with respect to this.

MR. LYNN: Well, they were not the only people voting on the matter.

REPRESENTATIVE HYDE: The day after the First Amendment was adopted by Congress, the Congress petitioned the president to issue a proclamation for prayer and thanksgiving. For anybody to say that Congress within twenty-four hours reversed itself and adopted a policy of hostility toward religion—the "wall of separation" that Justice Black erected in 1947—is unhistorical.

MR. LYNN: It is also not clear that the members of Cong

200 years ago fully recognized the implications of everything they did. That is why they sometimes spoke in general terms.

REPRESENTATIVE HYDE: You mean they did not know what they were doing in the First Congress? The first thing they did was to get a chaplain. They have opened their sessions every day, including today, with a prayer, as does the Supreme Court.

MR. DOERR: One can conclude from the deliberations of the 1780s and 1790s that a civil religion of sorts was in vogue. Men who were not orthodox Christians—for instance, Jefferson and Washington—made invocations to the Deity. But these were rather ceremonial examples of a civil religion that was in vogue at the time.

REPRESENTATIVE HYDE: What do you mean by a "civil religion"? There is a recognition of the fatherhood of God and the omnipotence of the Supreme Being in the Thanksgiving proclamations of Washington, his Farewell Address, and the Northwest Ordinance, where federal money was provided for churches and schools and for teaching the Indians. Our Founding Fathers were very concerned about the Indians. They provided money for priests and for churches so that the Indians could be taught Christianity and this took place closer to the time of the drafting of that First Amendment.

I am not disagreeing with the wisdom of what you are saying, but we are talking about what the Constitution means, what the framers understood it to mean, and who should say what it means today.

MR. DOERR: Madison, for example, was one of the primary architects of the Bill of Rights; as president he vetoed legislation passed by Congress that would have granted $10 worth of land in the Mississippi Territory to a Baptist church. His veto message makes clear that it was this sort of thing that the First Amendment was written to prohibit.

MR. BERNS: The ambiguity of this, I think, is reflected in the fact that what you have said is absolutely correct, and what I am about to say is also absolutely correct.

Here is Article III of the Northwest Ordinance that Representative Hyde referred to and that was adopted by the First Congress of the United States, the same Congress that proposed the First Amendment. And James Madison voted for this: "Religion, morality, and knowledge being necessary to good government and the happiness of mankind, schools and the means of learning shall forever be encouraged."

MR. DOERR: Was that not passed in 1787?

MR. BERNS: It was, of course originally passed by the Continental Congress in 1787, but it was immediately readopted to give it strength under the new Constitution—"readopted" is, I think, the exact phrase used by the First Congress of the United States. You see, the question I posed originally is this, and I think this is a fair statement of it: Do we agree or disagree that religion, morality, and knowledge are necessary to good government? If they are, then it might follow, and the First Amendment might have room for, a program of assistance on a nondiscriminatory basis, across-the-board, to all churches, all religions, all sects. That is my position, and I suspect it is Congressman Hyde's position.

MR. DALY: I mentioned earlier that the Senate defeated proposed amendments to the Constitution relating to voluntary prayer, both vocal and silent, in public schools. Neither was passed in the Senate, in spite of strong evidence in public opinion polls that a large majority of Americans favor some form of voluntary prayer in public schools. Should public polling play a paramount part in congressional and court decisions on religious issues?

MR. LYNN: No, it absolutely should not, though that was one

of the principal arguments used by those who would amend the Constitution. It was not an argument for what is *truly* voluntary prayer, however, because truly voluntary prayer is permitted in public schools now. No state school board official is going to come into a school lunchroom and try to stop someone from saying grace before he or she has lunch. No one is going to try to stop a basketball player from crossing himself before he takes the foul shot.

What the Senate was attempting to do was to prescribe that a minute be set aside at the beginning of each school day for the states to permit state-selected—not necessarily state-written, but state-selected—prayer, which would be sectarian prayer, which would be the establishment of religion, and which would be in very serious conflict, not just with the Establishment Clause as it exists today, but with the very notion of government neutrality in regard to religion.

REPRESENTATIVE HYDE: I have trouble being told about some particular religious philosophy being thrust on anybody, especially with the discipline that a school structure has. But by the same token, it seems incongruous that state legislatures and the federal Congress open every day with a prayer prescribed by somebody. I have never been asked for my selection by the chaplain who is paid with tax dollars; the Supreme Court says "God save the Constitution and this Court"; oaths are taken on Bibles. Everybody can pray one way or another in a structured manner except the kid in school. And I have problems with that.

MR. DOERR: When the Congress prays in the morning, they all do not stand up and recite the same prayer. Every member of Congress does not do this.

REPRESENTATIVE HYDE: We usually bow our heads and listen.

MR. DOERR: In your own state of Illinois, Mr. Hyde, school

prayer was done away with before any of us were born and the citizens of Illinois who have grown up since 1900 don't seem to be any the worse for it.

REPRESENTATIVE HYDE: We have some problems in Illinois—in Chicago. I will take you for a walk some evening and we will both pray we get out of the neighborhood. [Laughter]

MR. LYNN: Let's do it on the streets, not in the schools.

REPRESENTATIVE HYDE: Let's do it both places.

MR. LYNN: Silent prayer is another issue that means a great deal more than it might seem at first blush. There was an effort made to pass a silent prayer amendment to the Constitution that would have mandated essentially a moment of silent religious activity during the day, and the very selection of that mode of prayer is a dramatic step for any government to take.

Many people, of course, are offended by silent prayer. In fact, some of my more fundamentalist Christian friends believe that it is absolutely blasphemous to participate in silent prayer because prayer, in their tradition, must be oral for it to have any meaning. So the mere distinction between silent and vocal prayer has great theological significance and certainly is not something that the Congress ought to deliberate.

REPRESENTATIVE HYDE: I am thinking of introducing a bill to have young people in school pull out the old Declaration of Independence and read the part that states, "We hold these truths to be self-evident that all men are ... endowed by their Creator with certian unalienable Rights." I think it would be therapeutic, if not instructive, for students to cogitate on what our very Founding Fathers, way before the constitution, had in mind.

MR. DOERR: Every child may do this now—

REPRESENTATIVE HYDE: I understand that.

MR. DOERR: —in a public school.

REPRESENTATIVE HYDE: It is not done, and I think it ought to be done. You would not object to that would you, Mr. Doerr, to the Declaration of Independence being read in school?

MR. DOERR: If they do it every day for the purpose of having a religious exercise, it is objectionable, and it is trivializing the Declaration of Independence. It is degrading it.

REPRESENTATIVE HYDE: I think throwing it in the drawer and never reading it has trivialized it.

MR. DALY: Let me, if I may, come to the point of what has happened. If the facts are straight, there was evident in public polls a desire on the part of a great number of the public for voluntary vocal or silent prayer in public schools. It having been ordered by the Supreme Court that this was unconstitutional, the issue went to the Congress of the United States, where the power is vested for proposing changes to the Constitution, and it failed.

Now, does this not say that the American process worked perfectly here? There was deep consideration by the Congress, and the Congress did not overturn the ruling by the Supreme Court. But the ability to do so is there.

MR. LYNN: It is there, and in two and a half weeks of debate over the school prayer amendment, the Senate, in one of its finest hours recently, was able to defeat the amendment and decide to keep separation of church and state precisely where it is today.

REPRESENTATIVE HYDE: I agree with Mr. Lynn that the process really worked, and I think that is what our Founding Fathers intended. When you are going to change the Constitution, there is a formal and difficult process to go through. I would not say the right or the wisest result was obtained, but it was the democratic result. It was the way our Founding Fathers wanted it done, and I am proud of it in that sense.

But I would rather have that happen than have some judges decide, as Justice Jackson said, simply according to their prepossessions.

MR. DALY: Now, let's turn to the equal access issue that was before the Congress. This was the bill to guarantee access of student religious groups to school buildings on an equal basis with other student groups.

MR. BERNS: What interests me about that is the lack of public discussion as to the constitutional authority for the national government to decide whether the school system or the schools of, say, Ottumwa, Iowa, should or should not admit certain groups and give them access to school facilities to conduct their meetings. We have gone so far in this country that it is no longer a matter of discussion that the national government is assumed to have the authority to dictate that to Ottumwa. That is astonishing really.

Now, of course, the authority here in fact is tied to the federal government's giving out money; if one has the power to give money and promises or threatens to withhold it, one can do practically anything under this Constitution, and that raises problems.

As to the access question itself, what interests me is that the Supreme Court decided that religious groups could not have equal access to the use of a school building, but if the Communist party wanted access and the schools refused that access, the Court would rule in favor of the Communist party. Conclusion: Communists may have use of our public facilities; religious groups may not. That, I think, probably was not intended by James Madison.

MR. DOERR: You're right, Mr. Berns, that it is highhanded of

Congress to dictate policy to the school board in Ottumwa, Iowa, but the real issue is the gross abuse that could creep in or that would plainly be there.

There was nothing in that bill to prevent the proselytizing of children as young as eleven or twelve years, in the seventh grade, by outside adult missionaries. This sort of thing happens in many public schools. There was no safeguard against that in the bill. The sponsor of the bill had no interest in an amendment to the bill to provide these safeguards.

REPRESENTATIVE HYDE: My instinct was to support the equal access bill based on a libertarian theory that a school is a public building, paid for by public funds, and that it ought to be available to the public in an orderly fashion without chaos, so long as it is made available without discrimination.

So if the Moonies and the Hare Krishna want to come in, they are as entitled to exercise free speech as you or I, much as I would disagree with what they would say. But I do not see how we can shut the door to one group and not to another or shut the door to all groups under our Constitution.

MR. LYNN: This is a much more radical approach to religion in the public schools than even a moment of prayer, because it allows religious services; it allows doctrinal instruction as well as efforts to convert students right in the corridors and the classrooms of America's public schools.

MR. DALY: Can we discuss this in light of the fact that the Court has held that, at the public university level, equal access must be given to all groups if access is given to some. What is the great difference between this procedure now practiced in our universities and what is proposed in the public high schools?

MR. DOERR: There has to be a dividing line between people

who are old enough not to be easily indoctrinated and people who are young and immature. We have age requirements for acquiring a driver's license, for consuming alcohol, for getting married—

REPRESENTATIVE HYDE: And for learning about God, is that it?

MR. DOERR: We have institutions for learning about God. They are called churches and synagogues. The Supreme Court itself has said that the public schools may offer objective academic instruction about religion, and there is much of it going on that is perfectly respectable in our public schools.

REPRESENTATIVE HYDE: You require a level of maturity, then, before these ideas about religion may be foisted on young minds?

MR. DOERR: No. We draw lines. We will not even, for instance, let children into school until they are a certain age.

REPRESENTATIVE HYDE: Sex education for the little ones is okay, but not prayer.

MR. LYNN: There is one very important distinction that also makes a difference between the case of the University of Missouri and a junior high school in Illinois, and that is that the university was an open forum. It was truly open to every known organization.

REPRESENTATIVE HYDE: Equal access, in other words?

MR. LYNN: Equal access was truly there. And in America's public schools today, it is just as difficult—in fact, I would submit it's more difficult—to get a club to study Karl Marx than it is to get a club to study the Bible.

REPRESENTATIVE HYDE: I really would think the American

Civil Liberties Union would be pushing for equal access, even though there are ideas we do not agree with. Your proudest moment was also your toughest moment, and that was defending the right of the Nazis to march in public. I would not have done that. I think it would have caused a riot and, therefore, would be too inflammatory. But that took guts.

MR. LYNN: Again, in a public forum, such as a public park, we support it, but for the same reasons that we do not want religious worship services to occur in school, we do not want the Hitler youth movement to meet in school during school hours, because that would put the state's imprimatur or blessing on racially discriminatory activity in violation of the Constitution.

MR. DALY: Representative Hyde, tuition tax credits is an area of your particular interest. The issue is this: Some parents have decided that their children would receive a better education, perhaps including a deeper religious education, in private schools, both religious and nonreligious, but these parents would bear two burdens: tuition for private school and taxes for public schools. They argue that it is perfectly reasonable that there should be some kind of tuition tax credit. Would you speak to this issue?

REPRESENTATIVE HYDE: Ever since 1925, the Supreme Court has held that sending one's child to a parochial school fulfills the secular requirement of a public education, a good education, because the local board of education has certified that the child is getting a decent education.

If one can fulfill the state law requirement by sending one's child to a parochial school, I do not see the constitutional difficulty—we can argue the wisdom, though that is really another question, but I am prepared to argue that too—in providing tuition tax credits. This really says to the parent, you do not have to bear this double burden; we will let you keep some of your own money because your child is going to parochial school rather than public school.

It has been held by the Court that the money you put in the collection box on Sunday does not establish a religion. That has been held by the courts. I should not think tuition tax credits would establish a religion either.

MR. DOERR: You seem to think that there has not been a constitutional history on this. The Supreme Court, back in 1972 and 1973 and in subsequent decisions, examined several tuition tax credit programs from New York, Ohio, and New Jersey, and found them to be clearly unconstitutional. These programs were transferring money from the public treasury, for which we all are taxed, into the treasuries of religious institutions.

REPRESENTATIVE HYDE: With a tuition tax credit, Mr. Doerr, no money exchanges hands. The parent gets a deduction on his income tax.

MR. DOERR: That is not what the Supreme Court says.

REPRESENTATIVE HYDE: Those are the facts. You do not *give* money to anybody.

MR. DOERR: It is a fact that the public treasury goes down and the treasury of the parochial school goes up. It does not matter whether the dollar physically moved from one to the other.

REPRESENTATIVE HYDE: What about going to church on Sunday, putting a $20 bill in the collection box and then writing that off your income tax?

MR. DOERR: We all get deductions for contributions to religious and other charitable organizations, and that is provided across the board. But support for specifically religious institutions, the way tuition tax credits provide it, has been found by the Supreme Court to violate the Constitution.

REPRESENTATIVE HYDE: What is the essential constitutional difference between a deduction and a credit?

MR. LYNN: The essential constitutional difference is that the credit is closer to providing a direct subsidy to the institution and is worth much more.

MR. DOERR: There is a further infirmity. Tax aid, through tuition tax credits or vouchers or any other scheme, provides public support for the various kinds of invidious discrimination practiced by nonpublic schools—segregation according to creed, class discrimination, academic discrimination. There are a number of forms of discrimination that are practiced in nonpublic schools that would never be tolerated in public schools. Any form of federal or state aid to nonpublic schools means we are taxed to support those forms of discrimination.

REPRESENTATIVE HYDE: As long as the tax credit is allowed across the board to, for example, Methodist, Lutheran, Jewish, and Roman Catholic schools, it is my position that it is not unconstitutional. The second part of the First Amendment, which says that the free exercise of one's religion may not be prohibited, is violated by imposing a double burden on the parents who want to send their child to a parochial school.

MR. DOERR: By your logic, would you then support separate but equal schools for children of different races?

REPRESENTATIVE HYDE: Oh, no, no, not at all.

MR. DOERR: What's the difference between tax support for segregating kids by race and segregating them by religion?

REPRESENTATIVE HYDE: They are not segregated by religion. Every Roman Catholic parochial school in Chicago has a good percentage of non-Catholics and a mixture of races.

MR. DOERR: Oh, you can find some examples, but nationwide, nonpublic schools approach 100 percent religious homogeneity. The Catholic schools are somewhat more mixed than some of the others.

REPRESENTATIVE HYDE: Your facts are wrong.

MR. DALY: Let's move to the battle being fought on the issues of science education. On the one hand, some legislators and educators around the country argue that evolution remains but one theory of man's beginning and that the Biblical account of creation is another. They therefore conclude that both theories should be taught as part of students' science education. On the other hand, the argument is made that evolution is science and that the teaching of Biblical creationism only serves to advance religion and should not be taught as science.

MR. LYNN: This is another nearly bogus issue, a phony equality of treatment. There is nothing similar between the scientific theory of evolution and the religious theory of creationism. Creationism probably should be taught in public schools, but it should be taught in a comparative religion class where it belongs. It should not be in the public schools masquerading as science.

Science begins with observation, goes to experimentation, then tries to find the truth or falsity of the hypothesis that it develops. Creationism starts with the conclusion that everything was created by God 10,000 years ago, and then seeks to find miscellaneous bits of information from a variety of sciences to support the conclusion. That is not science.

REPRESENTATIVE HYDE: That is like a decision made by the Supreme Court; the Court begins with a result and then looks for ways to justify it. An educated person ought to know about the theory of creation as well as evolution and others, and the theories ought to be presented to the kids in a nondiscrimina-tory way. The teacher can say, "I prefer this because this is scientific." This is a leap of faith. There are people who believe in creationism. I think one's education is incomplete if he does not understand that.

MR. LYNN: But you do not think it should be taught as science in the biology books of the United States.

REPRESENTATIVE HYDE: I do not think it is unscientific to say there are those who believe that a force created something out of nothing, because science does not yet give us an answer to the question of the "uncaused cause."

MR. LYNN: No, but neither do biology textbooks about evolution. They leave that first cause, the uncaused cause, out of biology books for a good reason.

REPRESENTATIVE HYDE: One cay say, "now, take your science hat off and put your religion hat on; we're going to talk about creationism." But an educated person should know about both theories.

MR. DOERR: A teacher cannot take off his science hat and put on a religion hat. He has to be neutral.

REPRESENTATIVE HYDE: That is the sad thing for education.

MR. DOERR: Which religion hat would you have him put on in the school?

REPRESENTATIVE HYDE: All of the major religions: Islam, Judaism, Christianity—

MR. DOERR: This may be done now in social studies and

comparative religions classes. I am a former social studies teacher. I talked about religious issues in an academically neutral way. This can be done. It is being done by thousands and thousands of teachers.

REPRESENTATIVE HYDE: I know, but when one is talking about creationism in science, one should not have to recess and go down the hall—

MR. LYNN: But do you want every religious doctrine to be taught that has something to do with explaining man's relationship to the universe?

REPRESENTATIVE HYDE: Just the major ones.

MR. LYNN: But just a few moments ago, you said that we should not draw any distinctions about religion, that the Unification Church, the Baptist, the Methodist, the Catholic churches are all the same.

REPRESENTATIVE HYDE: You are talking about the time being spent teaching these things. I do not think there are that many theories about creationism. I do not think the Methodists and the Baptists have a different theory.

MR. LYNN: But there are not only Methodists and Baptists in the United States. There are, I think, 415 identifiable groups in this country today. There are hundreds of theories of Creation in the world.

MR. DOERR: The bottom line is that in a science class, the curriculum should be designed by scientists; in a Spanish class, it should be designed by experts in Spanish. Theologians should not be designing a curriculum just because they have an interest in a particular class.

MR. DALY: Let's move to the creche decision by the Supreme

Court if we may. Recently, the Court ruled, in the so-called *Pawtucket* case, that it is constitutional for a creche to be included in a holiday display on public grounds. Does this decision bother any of you in this context of church-state relations?

MR. BERNS: The *Pawtucket* case is a beautiful example of why the ACLU should keep its nose out of public business. That was a case in which the ACLU files a suit. The creche was not on public property; it was purchased with public funds. The case ought to have been declared moot before it got to the Supreme Court of the United States because the city sold the creche after it lost in the trial court, so there really was not any issue left.

Having said that nasty thing about the ACLU, let me try to defend it on more moderate grounds—defend my statement, that is to say, not the ACLU. The question ought to be raised as to why the Court granted standing in this particular case. As Mr. Lynn pointed out in the beginning, there are two parts to the First Amendment and, carried to extremes, the parts do, indeed, come into conflict with each other. To use my favorite example of this, we draft young men into the army and send them to remote places, and if we do not provide them with priests to administer the sacraments, we might be denying them free exercise of their religion. But, when we employ the chaplain, we might be violating the law with respect to an establishment.

My point here is that many of these cases ought not to be litigated, and so I would ask the Court to ask the ACLU, "What skin off your nose is it that we have this creche in Pawtucket?" By insisting on bringing this kind of a case to the Court, you might very well lose—as a matter of fact, you lost.

Now, what did you lose, and what have we lost because you lost that particular case? I would imagine that, in the past, many a city councilman, many a mayor has said, in effect, to some importunate constituent who asks for a religious display and so forth, "Charlie, you know doggone well we cannot do that. That gets into the First Amendment. The city cannot put creches on the top of the Palmolive building and so forth and so on." The consequences of the ACLU's pushing that suit and losing it is that it has deprived every mayor around the country of that response to all the Charlies, and there are lots of Charlies and lots of religions. Pretty soon the public world is going to be festooned with a variety of religious symbols.

MR. LYNN: One of the things that Justice Black said was that when you mix government and religion, you tend to destroy governments and degrade religion. In the *Pawtucket* case, we have the perfect example of the degradation of an important religious symbol because some "Charlie" in that state got his way with the mayor and the city council. Here, in fact, is the second-most important symbol of the Christian faith—the manger scene, the baby Jesus—in the middle of clowns, a talking wishing-well, an elephant, a blue bear, some reindeer, and the Santa Claus house.

I cannot imagine anything more degrading to this central symbol of Christianity than that scene. I am surprised that someone did not come out in the middle of the night and destroy this scene in the Pawtucket Square, not because of his constitutional objections, but because he thought it blasphemous.

MR. BERNS: The consequence of the ACLU filing that suit, and the Court granting standing to the ACLU, is that we are going to see that important symbol of Christianity surrounded by red-nosed reindeer all over this broad land. Thank you very much, ACLU.

MR. LYNN: We already were seeing it. It is clear from this suit and other suits around the country that involve the mixing of religious symbols with secular symbols. There are parents who are deeply religious and deeply Christian who take the matter of Christmas seriously, and who try their darndest to keep the secular meaning of Christmas and Santa Claus separate from the historic and religious meaning of the birth of Jesus Christ.

MR. DALY: We have covered several of the major areas of conflict with respect to the Constitution and religion and have come to the question-and-answer session. May I have the first question, please?

AUSTIN RANNEY, resident scholar, American Enterprise Institute: I would like to ask a public policy question, and direct it to all the members of the panel. What makes you think that state support of religion in any form will do good, and what evidence do you have for that; equally, what makes you think that state support of religion will do harm, and what evidence do you have for that?

MR. BERNS: It was the opinion of George Washington, of course, uttered in his Farewell Address, that there is a connection between morality, to use our word, and the viability of our republican institutions. Further testimony is provided by de Tocqueville, who developed this theme at great length, and indicated that the good health of the United States really did depend upon the continuation of certain habits. De Tocqueville probably provides the most thematic treatment of this subject available to us. The question he discussed was how—under this Constitution, under democratic auspices, when everything points to individualism and taking care of one's self—are all of us, all citizens of the United States, reminded that we have some responsibility toward others? I would suppose that religious education does, in fact, somehow, go some way to remind us of that.

Whether school prayers conducted under the auspices of a typical member of the National Education Association performs that function, I have my doubts.

REPRESENTATIVE HYDE: I am inclined to agree with Mr. Berns. One is tempted to say religion might not help, but it certainly could not hurt to have an objective, nondiscriminatory recognition of the fatherhood of God, if this agrees with a majority of people in a given community.

It is awfully hard to work on the brotherhood of man without some notion of the fatherhood of God—I, at least, have found it hard to prove the basic tenet, taken by itself, that all men are created equal. Clearly, human beings are different. There are smart ones and dumb ones, talented ones and klutzes. But if you do not consider the essentials, which are really God-given, you have problems proving our basic philosophy. What we need is an objective standard of morality, I think, rather than 235 million subjective standards of morality. So I, being very chary about abuses of the First Amendment and preferences on one religion over others, would like to see a return to the "fatherhood of God" notion.

MR. DOERR: Of course, there are many people of both genders who might feel that assigning a gender to God in that way is government taking a position on religion, and is therefore out of line.

REPRESENTATIVE HYDE: Oh, she does not mind. [Laughter.]

MR. DOERR: Okay, whatever. I think that Madison hit the nail on the head in his *Memorial and Remonstrance against Religious Assessments* in 1785, when he called attention to the fact that when government aids religion, it corrupts religion, it corrupts the clergy, it messes everything up. The evidence of history is that in those countries with a close union of church and state, where government subsidizes religion, promotes it, and tries to help it, there religion itself is corrupted and frequently becomes an ally of very bad politics.

In the American experience—I think Cardinal Cushing pointed this out—because we have implemented the principle of separation of church and state, we have had more religious tolerance and more religious freedom than any other society has ever known. When something ain't broke, as one of Murphy's corollaries has it, don't fix it. Church-state separation has been a great boon to our country. It is perhaps our most significant contribution to civilization. We should either leave it alone or try to enhance it.

MR. LYNN: Let me give you one very specific example of Mr. Doerr's point. In some schools in Michigan today, there is a program whereby public school teachers are paid to do part-time work by going into the parochial schools in Michigan and teaching subjects like advanced biology, music, and art appreciation, that would not otherwise be offered. But, in the process of sending those public school teachers into the private schools, in order to minimize the church-state conflict, all the religious pictures and the crucifixes are taken down from the walls of the classrooms that are used by those public school teachers. This takes what is sacred out of the school. The risk is that whenever one accepts benefits from Caesar, one may chip away a little piece of one's soul in the process.

Government support of religion tends to trivialize religion. That does not do any good for government and is bad for religion.

MR. BERNS: I should not like Mr. Doerr's response to remain as the final word on this question, "If it ain't broke, don't fix it." Let us not indulge the idea that the history of the United States is almost 200 unbroken years of complete separation of church and state. It certainly is not. There is more separation of church and state now than there was in the past. There certainly has been greater separation since the Supreme Court nationalized the First Amendment in 1947 and this whole issue became a national question. There certainly was more association of church and state on the state level, on the municipal level, in the past.

MR. DOERR: You are quite right, but I think we have been making progress, and it is to the good that we have greater separation now than we did 185 years ago.

REPRESENTATIVE HYDE: I am not satisfied that "it ain't broke," at least in terms of our society today. The narcotics problem is a tidal wave, whether we know it or not. We find it among athletes in sports and among all kinds of children in schools. As for pornography, we are so used to it now that it does not seem to do much—

MR. DOERR: What does that have to do with government meddling with religion?

REPRESENTATIVE HYDE: I am talking about how we have gotten away from such ideas as right and wrong, God, an objective standard of morality, and sanctions against doing wrong or doing anything other than what the nerve endings say will be immediately gratifying.

Society certainly is damaged, if not broken, and we should be looking for answers. A book on ethics isn't enough, in my opinion.

MR. LYNN: Justice Rehnquist recently said some frightening things about America today. He suggested that religious divisiveness is not a real problem in twentieth-century America. But in the process of debate over such volatile issues as school prayer and equal access we have seen the most intense demagoguery to support governmental intrusions into religious matters. This demagoguery has surpassed the lobbying for all kinds of unpopular causes that I have experienced in my ten years in Washington. At no other time have I received the hate mail and the threats that I received simply because I think that government should be out of the prayer-writing and prayer-selecting business.

Many of the valiant and courageous members of the United States Senate, who debated the school prayer amendment on the floor, received letters that were as disgraceful to legitimate and honest political debate as any I have ever seen on any issue. I think the potential for religious divisiveness exists; it occurs in communities around this country when religious clubs begin to meet in high schools.

We see neighbors pitted against neighbors, children pitted against children; we even see homes burned down, homes belonging to those courageous people in communities that protest religious activities in the public schools. We are a hair breadth away from true internecine, interreligious warfare in the United States. What we have seen happening in communities all over the country would certainly increase dramatically if we sent any constitutional amendment about church and state out for ratification by all the states.

A.E. DICK HOWARD, professor of law and public affairs, University of Virginia: The panel has made clear the role of the Supreme Court, especially since 1947, in importing the notion of the "wall of separation" into its First Amendment decisions on religion. In light of that, it is rather striking that the three most recent significant Supreme Court decisions have all been, in effect, accommodations; they have all upheld challenged state measures. The Minnesota case upheld tuition tax credits, the Nebraska case upheld the paying of chaplains, and the Pawtucket, Rhode Island case upheld the display of the creche. Do those three cases simply represent some marginal adjustment in the Court's thinking about the First Amendment, or are we now, all these years after *Everson,* seeing something that may portend a major adjustment toward more accommodation by states, and by government generally, to religious practices in the public arena?

MR. LYNN: I would not call what has happened simple accommodation, because there is lengthy, serious, and thoughtful case law about accommodating religious beliefs. At what point can one exempt individuals, on religious grounds, from laws of general applicability? The decisions you mentioned

have gone much further than that. They are not accommodations; they come dangerously close to what we mean by
establishment. The very absence of neutrality creates the
dangers of which I spoke—that is, the degrading of religion,
the trivializing of religion, and the creation of political warfare
among religious groups.

I think these have been bad decisions. Most of them,
thankfully, are very narrow decisions. It will depend, to some
degree, on the quality and the capabilities of the next few
appointees to the Supreme Court as to whether we will see a
trend toward establishment instead of a responsible recognition of accommodation.

REPRESENTATIVE HYDE: I disagree. They are fine decisions. The
absolute nature of the *Everson* decision is being recognized as
not having been based on scholarship. That case was not based
on how the First Congress and the framers felt and acted, or
on how the early presidents felt and acted, but was based on
what the Court felt the law ought to be at that time.

Whether these recent cases represent a significant shift in
the Court's thinking will depend on the personnel of the
Court, and that is the vice of letting the Court write
legislation or rewrite the Constitution according to their
prepossessions.

It is interesting that, about the turn of the century, the
Court was anathema to the progressive forces of America
because it was reactionary. Today, or recently, when it has been
a liberal court, it has been the darling of the progressive forces,
and the Congress, the elected body, is anathema.

ERVIN S. DUGGAN, Ervin S. Duggan & Associates: My
question is for Mr. Doerr, and has to do with the idea of a civil
religion. Would you tell us what you meant by that, and
perhaps the other members of the panel can comment on what
they think about the idea of a civil religion in America.

MR. DOERR: I wish I could. It is not that easy. Robert Bellah and others have written on this concept of a civil religion for a number of years now, and it has to do with a patriotic type of common piety that is not pinned to any specific doctrine. Many deeply religious people think that this sort of civil religion makes a mockery of true religion and is too easily used by politicians to distract attention from the country's real problems. I am afraid that I have not seen the concept of civil religion precisely defined.

MR. BERNS: Strictly speaking, a civil religion would be a religion recognized by the city, if you will, and the subject, of course, has been treated by people like Rousseau.

ELIZABETH LITTLE, Concerned Women for America: Mr. Lynn, you stated that you are against any doctrinal instruction of children. Many parents extremely dislike their children being taught situation ethics in school with public tax money. These parents believe that there are intrinsic rights and intrinsic wrongs, and they find this philosophy of situation ethics quite in conflict with their moral standards. What rights do you think these parents have?

MR. LYNN: Parents have a right to expect that, in a class dealing with questions of values, students will be taught that some people believe there are different values depending on the situations, and other people believe there are fundamental and correct positions of right and wrong on the great moral questions of the day. Any school not teaching that both of these views are responsible ways to do moral analysis is a school that needs a little help and whose teachers need a little help. But I resist the idea that seems implicit in your question that somehow situation ethics has been prescribed as the national or state religion, or that secular humanism or some other phrase reflecting a point of view about values has been established as the national religion. It has not. None of this has happened. Courses in ethics and in processes of moral reasoning are appropriate in the schools and should reflect the many, many dozens of varieties of ethical thinking.

MR. BERNS: I am a member of the National Council of the Humanities, and the question of support from federal tax dollars comes up quite frequently regarding situation ethics or some variety of it, and the teaching of such at the seventh-grade level, for example. I would prefer to have children at that level told, with some authority behind it, that it is wrong to murder another human being or to steal from that other human being, et cetera, than to have these subjects introduced as debatable propositions, and I think this is a fair way of stating it. If we are concerned, as the Supreme Court is, about the difference between older and younger students, and about what might be done in colleges with older people and not done with younger children because younger children are more impressionable, I think that carries over here, too. I want to impress on young people that murdering other human beings is not debatable.

MR. LYNN: When you get beyond those two examples—murdering and stealing—what is the basis for the moral absolutes you would teach?

MR. BERNS: I absolutely recognize the problem you are getting at. We have to avoid anything that leads us in the direction of Ian Paisley or the Ayatollah Khomeini. I do not minimize the problem at all, Mr. Lynn.

MR. DOERR: Of course, teaching values in school is not a simple matter of one, two, three, this is the truth, and it cannot be questioned. I think teachers have a more sophisticated approach to the situation. You do not say a murder is wrong simply because I say so or because it is in the Ten Commandments. It is appropriate for a teacher to encourage a class of kids to discuss why a murder is wrong, why stealing is wrong, and—

MR. BERNS: You can try that with me, Mr. Doerr, and I can figure out some reasons why those things are not wrong: I suspect a ten-year-old can too.

REPRESENTATIVE HYDE: I just spent some time with Senator Jeremiah Denton of Alabama after having read his book *When Hell Was in Session*. He spent seven and a half years in a prison camp in North Vietnam, four of those years in solitary confinement. And I got from that book the fact that he would never have survived without a strong religious faith.

That does not cut one way or the other in our discussion except to say that his religious faith proved valuable. Situation ethics would not have helped him survive while he was in solitary confinement or being tortured. His religious faith did. I note that the military academies compel attendance at religious services if you belong to a given religion.

MR. DOERR: No, they do not. The federal court of appeals in Washington several years ago ruled that the service academies cannot compel students to attend worship.

REPRESENTATIVE HYDE: We disagree.

MR. LYNN: I believe it is wrong to say that one cannot have a strong religious faith and still believe in situation ethics. There is great debate among Christians as to whether Jesus himself was a situationalist.

REPRESENTATIVE HYDE: Cardinal Newman asked, "Who was ever consoled in time of real trouble by the small beer of literature and music?" and I am just suggesting a strong religious faith can save your life sometimes.

MAURY ABRAHAM, Unitarian Universalist Association: I would like to ask the panelists to comment on the recent appointment of a U.S. ambassador to the Holy See.

REPRESENTATIVE HYDE: I do not think it is any big deal, frankly; it is a change in title. I know it offended many people who think the naming of an ambassador to a religion is a violation of separation of church and state. I do not know if it was worth all of the fuss that it created; I do not think it is an earth-shaking event.

MR. LYNN: It certainly gives added credibility to the notion that one religion is favored—the Roman Catholic faith—because we do not have an ambassador going to the World Council of Churches in Geneva, Switzerland serving as a representative of the United States.

REPRESENTATIVE HYDE: I would vote for that if we did.

MR. LYNN: Would you? Even the World Council of Churches?

REPRESENTATIVE HYDE: Sure.

MR. LYNN: The appointment of the ambassador also gives a favored status to the Roman Catholic church because this makes it much easier for that religious organization to speak to the United States government through the Department of State. It gives them access that is not given to any other faith in the United States.

REPRESENTATIVE HYDE: Do you mean the apostolic delegate, now that he is an ambassador, will make any difference at all?

MR. LYNN: He may, and I think another problem is created for American Catholics. I wonder if this will not lead U.S. officials to inappropriate meddling with papal representatives to influence policy being made by the American bishops. That also worries me.

MR. DOERR: Another matter that concerns many Catholics is the fact that part of the justification for naming an ambassador to the Holy See is that it would enable the U.S. government to tap the intelligence network that the Catholic church allegedly has. What this tells revolutionaries, the Shining Path movement in Peru, for instance, is that from now on Catholic priests, missionaries, and nuns may be spying for the CIA, and they may become fair targets. This establishment of relations with the Holy See may actually endanger the lives of Catholic missionaries working in the third world, according to some Catholics.

MR. BERNS: I doubt whether the appointment of this ambassador makes the Roman Catholic church the established church of the United States. In fact, we already have an established church in the United States; it's the Old Order Amish, because the Old Order Amish are entitled, as no other group is, to disobey a law that is a valid criminal statute, thanks to the Supreme Court of the United States in *Wisconsin v. Yoder*.

The interesting thing is that in the name of the Free Exercise Clause, the Court has gone to astonishing lengths. Freedom of religion manifests itself in our time as demands for exemption from laws applying to everyone. That is what Yoder did. He is an Old Order Amish man who refused to send his child—probably with good reason—to the local public high school. [Laughter.] There was a criminal statute under which he was fined $5.00, I think—talk about small beer—and the Supreme Court allowed this to come before it and ruled in Yoder's favor because he was Old Order Amish. The Court then went on to say that this did not hold for any other group, just Old Order Amish. That is the established church in the United States, Old Order Amish.

MR. LYNN: If you do not think that is a legitimate free exercise issue, then what possible meaning does the Free Exercise Clause have?

MR. BERNS: Jefferson gave us the formula for that.

MR. LYNN: If one cannot be exempted from laws because of religious belief, what else is there to the Free Exercise Clause?

MR. BERNS: It is a fundamental principle of American government that no one, because of his religious faith, shall be exempted from the necessity to obey valid criminal statutes; once you start down the road of exemption, there will be a proliferation of sects in this country, given the opposition of churches to paying taxes and all.

MR. LYNN: A compelling government interest has been raised in those cases, and we have not seen the floodgates open to every cult, sect, and faith in America because of the Old Order Amish. We have a very responsible decision that puts some meat into the Free Exercise Clause; some of us believe that the meat is necessary in both the Establishment Clause and the Free Exercise Clause.

REPRESENTATIVE HYDE: Didn't Timothy Leary try to start the League for Spiritual Development, and didn't that involve the use of LSD? The courts did not uphold that.

MR. LYNN: But the courts have upheld the use of peyote by the Native American church because such use is central to the very religious beliefs of that organization.

MR. BERNS: Jefferson's formula covered this. It is no denial for the Free Exercise Clause; one can pray and so forth, but one must obey the law. That's it. We cannot afford to take the route that allows someone to exempt himself. If I could refuse, as a Marine, to go to Lebanon because I refuse to shoot my Muslim brothers there, what sort of an army would we have? Or, to be precise, what sort of Marine Corps would we have if that sort of thing is allowed, Mr. Lynn? No thank you.

MR. LYNN: Do you want the man who does not want to fight and who will not kill his Muslim brethren to be in Lebanon next to you in the foxhole? I suspect you do not.

MR. BERNS: I do not, but I would prefer that that exemption be established by congressional statute. Somebody in the Marine Corps who does not want to go fight where the Marine Corps has to fight ought not to be in the Marine Corps.

MR. LYNN: He should be discharged. This kind of incident just occurred, and discharge was sought.

MR. BERNS: Mr. Lynn, is the ACLU going to litigate that case?

MR. LYNN: We are not, to my knowledge, involved in that specific case, but we have been involved in cases for the past fifty years on the question of conscientious objection to military service. As you know, it is a very lively issue yet today because the Congress has failed to provide the opportunity in the current draft registration system for conscientious objectors to indicate that they are conscientious objectors and do not wish to be considered a part of that pool of persons eligible, willing, and able to go to fight whenever their government calls them.

REPRESENTATIVE HYDE: But you know they will have an opportunity to declare their conscientious objection if and whenever we reestablish the draft, which may or may not happen.

MR. LYNN: If the Congress decides to preserve that right, which the courts have said is just a matter of legislative grace.

MR. DALY: This concludes another public policy forum presented by the American Enterprise Institute for Public Policy Research. On behalf of AEI, our hearty thanks to our distinguished and expert panelists, Mr. Walter Berns, Representative Henry J. Hyde, Mr. Edd Doerr, and the Reverend Barry Lynn, and also our thanks to our guests and experts in the audience for their participation.

FOUR

Spiritual Leadership and the Abortion Crisis

A BORTION IS THE PARAMOUNT moral issue of the age—the "single issue" that commands the concern and time and energy of everyone who cherishes human life. The prolife movement is the archetypal "single issue movement." It is a coalition of Americans of diverse beliefs, backgrounds, races, and political loyalties who have come together in the selfless effort to end the holocaust of the unborn in our country.

The prolife movement has grown in numbers and in influence in recent years. The prolife position is being received with new respect in our society, and we can even entertain the serious possibility that a reconstituted Supreme Court will reverse its disastrous *Roe v. Wade* decision in the near future.

It is ironic, therefore, that the "single issue" focus of the prolife movement would be challenged at a time when the movement's success is largely attributable to its clear goals. It is doubly ironic that the challenge would be mounted on "ethical" grounds, and that its source would be the Catholic bishops of the United States—a group of cherished friends and supporters of the prolife movement for many years. I am referring to the concept of the "seamless garment" of prolife positions. Here I will explain why the "seamless garment" notion disheartens me and threatens the prolife movement.

Then I will outline what I think it will take to achieve final success.

The seamless garment was popularized by Cardinal Joseph Bernardin of Chicago in 1983. As chairman of the U.S. Catholic bishops' Committee for Pro-Life Activities, Cardinal Bernardin has shown himself to be determined to expand the concept of "prolife" beyond mere opposition to abortion, to include opposition to war, opposition to capital punishment, and a generalized support for the liberal agenda. He has fashioned the now famous metaphor by insisting that these "life issues" form a "seamless garment," and that the truly prolife position is one which maintains a "consistent ethic" on these issues. The overwhelming majority of American bishops have expressed support for this view.

On examination, however, the seamless garment has proven to be somewhat elusive. Archbishop Bernard Law of Boston made an important distinction when, on August 7, 1984, he told the Knights of Columbus that "however weighty the urgency of life related issues such as the right to life of the unborn and the spiraling nuclear arms race, one thing must be clearly noted: nuclear holocaust is a frightening possibility but the holocaust of abortion is a present cruel reality and fact."

On February 10, 1985, Cardinal Bernardin supported Archbishop Law's view by writing in the *Chicago Catholic,* "abortion is not a 'potential threat' as is nuclear warfare, but a holocaust now realized and probably underestimated. For that reason, I fully agree that abortion demands priority attention."

In October, 1984, however, Cardinal Bernardin was less than explicit about this priority when he spoke at Georgetown University and spelled out his intent (and thus that of the American bishops) on the consistent ethic one must adopt to be rightly credentialed as prolife.

He referred to his famous speech nearly a year earlier at Fordham University where he first announced the "seamless garment" thesis and stated that "I am more convinced than ever that the ethic of the seamless garment is the best analytical setting in which to develop a posture in defense of human life."

One cannot deny a certain plausibility to the cardinal's ideas. Implicitly, however, he advances the classic charge leveled against the antiabortion movement since its earliest days—that of "single issue" politics.

This epithet was unheard of in the halcyon days of the civil rights movement and antiwar protesters, nor would one dare apply it to environmentalists or Equal Rights Amendment supporters today. If the most brilliant political candidate since Franklin Roosevelt were to come along and be "correct" on every controversial issue but one—say he believed in some degree of press censorship—does anyone doubt that single issue would doom him in the eyes of the same media that endlessly deplores "single issue politics"?

Some issues are so difficult, so controversial, and so furiously resisted that one such issue can command all the physical and moral energy a person may possess. I suggest in a nation where one and a half million abortions a year are performed, the fact that some people assign a higher priority to what they conceive as the *real* "clear and present danger," the extermination of innocent preborn children, does not render them less "prolife" than the bishops themselves.

All can agree that peace is a desirable goal. We are, nonetheless, far from agreement on the best means to reach this goal. The pacifist has one way, the hawk another, and the moderate will search for a middle ground. All are respectable views and may be most sincerely held. But disagreement over the means does not invalidate their moral legitimacy.

I have never met anyone who was *for* war or poverty. I have met a lot of thinking people who agree on the bishops' goals, but disagree on the means to attain these goals. These disagreements are rational intelligent judgments founded in as much good will and sincerity as those of the bishops.

With due respect, I resent being charged with inconsistency concerning the "life issues" because I believe in the private sector more than the public sector as the great strength of our country and our society. The liberal welfare agenda hasn't seemed to solve the riddle of poverty, and those of us who wish to try other approaches are no less concerned about alleviating poverty than those who always opt for a federal solution.

If anything is ironical about the seamless garment, it is that *exclusion* will be the likely result of its use. We should be seeking to *include* certain prominent senators and congressmen within the active antiabortion ranks. However, by reducing opposition to abortion to the level of opposition to capital punishment (is there no essential difference between innocent life and "guilty life"?), antiwar activism (domestic, of course; we can't all picket the Kremlin) and more and bigger federal programs to solve poverty (the only valid charity is collective rather than individual) we dilute our moral capital and introduce new political controversies.

The seamless garment, literally applied, provides too many political leaders with camouflage to cover up their failure to aggressively oppose legalized abortion. If Geraldine Ferraro and Mario Cuomo won't buy the seamless garment, who will?

If a psychic ray existed that could probe through the jargon and rhetoric that surrounds the abortion debate, I suspect you would find the single most distancing feature between the establishment elite and the essentially socially conservative prolife forces to be cultural distaste.

It is a rare discussion on this topic that doesn't produce a spate of patronizing disparagement towards "those people," best symbolized by the public figure at once the most successful defender of the preborn and the most hated by the establishment, Senator Jesse Helms of North Carolina. When some people get tired of vilifying Senator Helms they turn their cannon on Jerry Falwell. But make no mistake, the same cultural divide also separates this elite from President Reagan as well, and no amount of intellectual or evidentiary argument can overcome the pervasive and enduring cultural animosity that underlies this struggle.

When Senators Kennedy, Moynihan, and Leahy support the

federal defunding of abortion and cosponsor a constitutional amendment to reverse *Roe v. Wade,* I will gladly concede efficacy to the strategy of the seamless garment. I shall not, however, hold my breath.

The indictment of inconsistency so often leveled at many prolifers achieved its most pungent expression from liberal Congressman Barney Frank of Massachusetts, who was admiringly quoted by columnist Mary McGrory in the *Washington Post* on January 27, 1985:

> They know they are faulted because they focus so obsessively on the child in the womb and have so little to say for the child in need. They have heard Barney Frank's famous barb about the administration's concern for children— "Begins with conception, ends with birth."

This "famous barb" is a sure laugh-getter but its capsule disparagement of antiabortion activists is just plain wrong. In the January, 1985 edition of the *Atlantic* magazine Nat Hentoff, who by acclamation belongs in the Civil Libertarian Hall of Fame, wrote a strong article on "The Awful Privacy of Baby Doe," wherein he severely criticized the "management option" of death often chosen for infants born with Down's Syndrome, cerebral palsy, and spina bifida. A most interesting part of this article deals with the congressional debate on legislation seeking to provide these already born members of the human family with at least ordinary medical care, the same as a nonhandicapped citizen is entitled to receive.

Hentoff says, "Liberals led the debate against those provisions on the House floor, and conservatives, by and large, supported the measure." He cites me as an "unabashed Tory" and quotes my remarks in debate:

> The fact is, that . . . many children . . . are permitted to die because minimal routine medical care is withheld from them. And the parents who have the emotional trauma of

being confronted with this horrendous decision, and seeing ahead a bleak prospect, may well not be, in that time and at that place, the best people to decide. . . . I suggest that a question of life or death for a born person ought to belong to nobody, whether they are parents or not. The Constitution ought to protect that child. . . . Because they are handicapped, they are not to be treated differently than if they were women or Hispanics or American Indian or Black. [Their handicap] is a mental condition or a physical condition; but by God, they are human, and nobody has the right to kill them by passive starvation or anything else.

Hentoff continues:

On the key vote concerning this section of the bill Congresswoman Geraldine Ferarro joined other renowned liberals in the House in voting against protections for handicapped babies, though most, to be sure, said they were supporting the right of parents to make life-or-death decisions about their infants and opposing government interference in that process. Among the others in opposition were such normally fierce defenders of the powerless as Peter Rodino, Henry Waxman, Don Edwards, Barney Frank, John Conyers, Thomas Downey, Charles Rangel, Robert Kastenmeier, Gerry Studds, George Crockett, and Barbara Mikulski.

The brilliant columnist Joseph Sobran, in a devastating critique entitled "Abortion and the American Bishops," raises further troubling questions about the seamless garment metaphor:

Why didn't the Cardinal, or the bishops in general, raise traditional *Catholic* "life issues," to call them that, such as those concerned with the very transmission of life? Much might be said about sexual morality—about contraception, divorce, pornography, fornication, homosexuality. The virtue of chastity would bear mention, not only for its intrinsic value but in light of the ubiquitously visible consequences of unchastity. One suspects, however, that these themes would jeopardize the sort of "credibility" the hierarchy pines for. Certainly the bishops have said little, in their highly-publicized recent statements on nuclear war and economics, to disturb secular liberalism. It takes very little political sophistication to know that the "seamless garment" and "single-issue" arguments are directed exclusively against the more conservative and orthodox members of the Catholic Church. The most striking aspect of these arguments is that they are never—never—applied even-handedly. Cardinal Bernardin doesn't address his demand for a "consistent ethic" to liberals. If he meant it seriously, however, he couldn't fail to do so. He would certainly warn them that they could not (credibly) oppose war and poverty *unless they also opposed abortion*. He has said not a single word to this effect; and until he does so, his whole metaphor of the seamless garment will deserve to be regarded (as it already is) as a rhetorical stratagem for the liberal cause. It serves precisely to "dilute" the anti-abortion position. It has no other effect whatever.

Father Francis Canavan, S.J., of Fordham tells us:

The more often those who exercise authority in the name of Jesus Christ act like politicians in a pluralistic liberal democracy, the more they engender, not open revolt, but something that in the long run is even worse. That is a chronic, low-grade infection of disillusionment, cynicism, apathy, and loss of interest in the Church and her works.

This is not the kind of phenomenon that makes tomorrow's headlines, and it may take some years to register in the statistics of sociological surveys. But its effect on the

Church is nonetheless real; it means that the Church loses the confidence of her people.

Very few senators and members of Congress can meet the requirements of the seamless garment in its strictest formulation. In fact, the leftist *National Catholic Reporter* in 1984 named only three senators and seven House members who are entitled to be called "prolife" under this definition. What are the consequences of this? Since most politicians fall short, a voter who believes the consistent ethic garment is really seamless can be justified in supporting a candidate who supports abortion funding, on the ground that this lapse alone is not disqualifying.

The bishops must know that moving the Democratic party towards an antiabortion stance will take a miracle and since they much value the liberal agenda, they have insisted that voters consider a candidate's views on arms control, the economy, welfare, and Central America, as well as abortion. Is it any wonder that abortion, as a crucial issue, gets lost in the shuffle?

I have a suggestion for the highest and best use for the seamless garment. When blood is flowing (and in America an abortion occurs every 20 seconds), you urgently need to apply a tourniquet.

I would suggest our bishops take their seamless garment and use it *now* to stop the shedding of the innocent blood of those defenseless preborn who, like each of us, is made in the image and likeness of God.

If they do this, the bishops would be exercising effective prolife leadership.

Effective, courageous, clear-headed leadership is something the prolife movement needs. Our strength is in our grass-roots organization—the hundreds and thousands of local groups encompassing countless dedicated men and women who do the hard work of education, lobbying, and fundraising. The heroes and heroines of the movement are the sidewalk counselors who take the verbal abuse of the establishment as they witness to the sanctity of human life on the streets outside abortion clinics.

The movement as a whole, however, has been weakened by disunity. It is a movement that has attracted many strong personalities and such individuals disagree on many matters of tactics and strategy. We need the strong personalities, but we also need leaders with the talent to forge a common vision and the courage to speak out for the unborn at times when courageous speech can be costly.

In Congress, the institution I know best, we have a desperate need for men and women who will speak out for life. We particularly need women to take this issue and run with it. I take my hat off to three women in Congress, two of them Democrats, who are fearless in their defense of the unborn. They are Mary Rose Oakar of Ohio, a liberal Democrat; Marilyn Lloyd of Tennessee, a conservative Democrat; and Barbara Vucanovich of Nevada, a Republican. There are many other members of Congress who should be as bold as these three.

Grass-roots activity is the way to make public officials bold. Some of us are ideological on this issue; we are driven to oppose abortion for reasons of conscience. However, the intensity of most congressmen's feelings on this issue reflects the intensity of the feelings of people back home in his district. Organize locally. Keep the pressure on. We need the right people who care enough to put energy into the local prolife organization. We need, in a word, leadership.

Effective local organization will help those in public office understand that they will not suffer politically by speaking out for life. President Reagan has not suffered for his outspoken prolife views. Neither will our governors, state legislators, senators, and congressmen suffer for defending life. If our public officials will not see this as an important issue, we need to elect men and women to public office who do.

We should put as much energy into providing alternatives to

abortion as we do into politics and education. Abortions happen because women think an abortion will solve the problem their pregnancy has caused them. They are wrong, tragically wrong, to think that abortion solves any problem, but the problems are real nevertheless. We need to reach out to these women in love with all the help we can muster.

Local prolife organizations should also take an interest in the way biology is taught in the schools. There are many signs that science is being taught more fairly. We are making progress in putting aside the myth that unborn babies are less than full members of the human family. With an accurate presentation of the facts of fetal development to students, the biological question about the humanity of the unborn should be settled rather quickly.

That will leave us with the values question: what value do we ascribe to human life? The battle over this question is the titanic struggle of our time. It transcends the abortion issue. The values question lies at the heart of the growing acceptance of infanticide in the past decade. The value of human life is being weighed and measured by policy makers as we live longer and the American population grows older. We have already heard Governor Richard Lamm of Colorado talk about older people's duty to die. Unless we as a society understand that human life is priceless, measures to eliminate old people might become respectable just as abortion is respectable.

Here we need prolife leadership from our spiritual leaders. Our bishops and pastors and denominational bodies should be insisting that a human society not governed by the Ten Commandments is a society governed by the laws of animal husbandry.

We are going to win the struggle over values. More and more Americans are coming forward, willing to be considered cultural lags by the Gucci Bolsheviks who dominate the society pages. It is becoming culturally fashionable to protect the defenseless unborn. And rightly so, for the prolife side is the winning side. Biology is on our side. Science is on our side. Tradition and history are on our side. So we can go forth with confidence because we have all these allies and because we do work that is dear to God's heart.

A concluding word about the religion and politics debate generally. I enjoy the tumult and turmoil of politics and I would be the last person to deplore partisanship in public life. But I think that spiritual leaders who plead for a "consistent ethic of life" that strongly resembles a liberal social agenda and conservatives like me who find such ideas offensive should go as far as we can to lay politics aside.

We conservatives need to learn to be sensitive to the dispossessed of this world and to understand that self-help remedies often are not enough. There is a legitimate role for government in providing assistance to people who desperately need it. We need to recognize that we are not buying the entire liberal agenda when we acknowledge that government in today's society needs to do more than deliver the mail and defend the country. Conservatives are learning this. But we have not completely learned this lesson yet.

For their part, our spiritual leaders need to develop more respect for people who disagree with them on the means to attain the ends we all share—peace, the alleviation of poverty, and greater freedom in the world. They also should give first priority to seeking spiritual solutions to the horrendous problems we face. We are not going to find the way to peace and freedom in the fever swamps of politics, but rather in a renewed spiritual awareness and commitment. That is why efforts to exclude religion from public life are cutting us off from the spiritual solutions to our public problems.

About six months after the 1984 presidential election I ran into the Reverend Jesse Jackson in O'Hare Airport and sat with him on a flight from Chicago to Washington, D.C. We talked. Mr. Jackson told me he had been visiting public schools in the Washington area. In most places, he found himself talking about drugs.

At one school, not an inner city school, Mr. Jackson asked the kids who were on drugs to come down in front. About 100 students came forward. It was a highly emotional scene. The kids were crying, both those up front and those in the audience. The school authorities were nonplussed.

"We've tried everything," Mr. Jackson said he told the students. "Drug education, threats, lectures, police—everything except one thing—God. Maybe that's the only place we have left to turn. Let's pray to God that you will all be delivered from drugs." Everyone held hands while Mr. Jackson led the students and teachers in prayer, even though he knew that what he was doing was probably illegal in the United States of America.

I was very moved by this story. I think Jesse Jackson is a gifted preacher and spiritual leader and I hope he puts this great gift to use in the great causes. The great causes are not who becomes the mayor of Chicago or the chairman of the Democratic National Committee or even president of the United States. The great causes are finding ways for generations of young people to get free of drug addiction. The great cause of our time is finding a way out of the spiritual malaise that grips society.

Our society is on its knees—not in prayer, but as a result of the social bludgeoning of teenage pregnancies, divorce, the plague of drugs, the explosive criminality that makes our cities dangerous to walk in. I believe that our society desperately needs spiritual renewal led by men and women of deep faith who can lead us to a recognition of the fatherhood of God. That is a cause worth working and praying for.

FIVE

Ethics in Conflict: Quality of Life vs. Sanctity of Life

On June 4, 1983, I delivered the commencement address at Thomas Aquinas College in Santa Paula, California. Aquinas is a small, excellent, Catholic liberal arts college. The atmosphere of serious Christian scholarship, the reverence with which the eighteen graduates, the faculty, and administration approached their faith, the beautiful setting, and the sense of new beginnings that surround a commencement all combined to move me deeply. I spoke extemporaneously about the value of human life. This is an edited version of my remarks.

ON GRADUATION DAY, mixed feelings pervade graduates. They are consumed with relief that the four years are over; regret that they haven't done a little better; sadness at the fact that the friends they have made will not be as accessible to them in the future; hope that the future will be as bright as it promises to be today; and pride—understandable pride—at a significant accomplishment.

I too have my mixed feelings. I am indeed intimidated by looking at your curriculum and seeing that you have not only read the great books but you can pronounce the authors' names and that you understand them.

I am trying to think of the word—the unique word—to describe the presumption that I feel in addressing such educated people and I think the only word that I can conjure up is *chutzpah*. It takes a lot of *chutzpah* for me to be here and to address you.

The Need to Restate the Obvious

George Orwell wrote a review in 1939 of a book by Bertrand Russell in which he said that the society had sunk now to the level that the intellectual must be content with restating the obvious. As you get older and as you engage in your careers, you will find that some of the basic, fundamental things that you have learned here so well are forgotten, and that restating the obvious sometimes is a very signal service to humanity.

Human Nature Remains the Same

The future is yours, of course, because you are graduates. But the past is with you and is yours as well. And the past is very, very important. George Will, in writing about Napoleon, said that Napoleon ricocheted through civilization, making so much history and so many orphans, because he wasn't encumbered by the educated person's sense of limitations.

Education provides you with a sense of limitations as well as a sense of boundless optimism. History, of course, should never be neglected because the constant—whether it is in the Dark Ages or the days of St. Clotilde, from then until now—is human nature. Human nature has always remained the same with the same limitations and the same glorious potential.

Sanctity of Life

Today in the world there are many conflicts. You were born at a very significant time. No one can afford to be mediocre, as

Pius XII said some years ago. You were born into a time of immense turmoil and here in our country, which God has blessed so much. We are seeing this struggle take the shape of the conflict between the sanctity of life ethic and the quality of life ethic.

The Judeo-Christian notion is that all men and women are important and significant and equal in the essentials—in that each of us is created by Almighty God, each of us is the object of God's redemptive love, and each of us is accountable to God for our stewardship. We are all equal in that and therefore there is no life unworthy to be lived. Every life is worthy to be lived because we are equal in the essentials.

The Quality of Life Philosophy

You contrast against that the ascendant philosophy of the quality of life, that a child is not to be brought into the world unless he is a wanted child, that the quality of life is as important as the very existence of life. This ascendant notion has, to my dismay, captured even our courts.

The question in the case of abortion is whether or not a child shall be aborted because the parents for one reason or another don't want it, or for economic reasons cannot cope with this situation. I refer to such children as the innocently inconvenient.

It used to be that the proponents of abortion as a solution to the unwanted pregnancy would deny the humanity of the unborn: "Well, it is just a blob. It is just a bunch of randomly multiplying cells." Then, when they would admit that indeed it was living tissue, they deny personhood to it, they deny humanity to it.

They Pretend It Isn't Human

Have you ever been in a highrise building where the elevator goes 11 ... 12 ... 14 ... 15? You say: "Where is the thirteenth floor?" and people say, "Well, there isn't one." You say "Yes, there is a thirteenth floor. They just don't call it that." They call it the fourteenth floor because, for reasons of superstition, people don't like to have offices or spend the night on the thirteenth floor. Everyone pretends it isn't there—but everyone knows it is.

Well, that's the unborn, the humanity of the unborn. They pretend it isn't human. They pretend it is not of any value, that animals have more value: a snail darter, a whale, a baby harp seal.

Did you ever stop to think a blade of grass has more protection in the law than an unborn child? "Don't step on the grass." "Don't trespass." It is certainly very true. But the unborn child has less value than a used piece of Kleenex under the Supreme Court's decision. Suddenly we are confronted with another aspect of this struggle between the quality of life and the sanctity of life.

Nontreatment as Treatment

Baby Boy Doe was born in Bloomington, Indiana, a little child with Down's syndrome and a digestive problem that required a simple surgical procedure. Without surgery he could not eat food and get nourishment, but with the surgical procedure connecting the esophagus and the stomach, the child could be nourished and survive. His parents decided they did not want the baby to survive: better that the baby should not live than live with Down's syndrome and a degree—maybe great, maybe not so great—of mental retardation. And so they said, "Don't perform the surgery."

That was presented to the parents as a management option: nontreatment as treatment. The hospital—a university hospital—decided they wanted some protection. They went into court and got a court order from the highest court in Indiana sanctioning this nontreament of this little baby in the crib, who starved to death under court order surrounded by these healers, these curers, these alleviators of pain.

To add another dimension to the tragedy, there were six families that wanted to adopt the baby. Six families said: "Give us your little Down's syndrome child. We're not worried about a Down's syndrome child. They can teach us about love. They're not selfish, they're not greedy, they're not bad. They're incapable of sin really. They can teach us something, they're a claim on our love. Give us your child."

No—we won't permit an adoption, we won't permit the surgery, and we let it starve to death. We let it—notice how I use the word *it*—let *him*, let this little baby boy, die. We wouldn't even give him the dignity of a name.

You see, part of the abortion mentality is: Dehumanize, dehumanize, call them fetuses, call them the products of conception. Don't humanize this little innocently inconvenient member of the human family because he doesn't measure up to the quality of life ethic. He can't pass the physical or the mental examination that we elite have determined as a condition precedent to admittance into the family of life.

Childhood Euthanasia

So you wipe away all of the nonsense, all of the sophistry about being human: is it alive? when does human life begin? It was alive. It wasn't animal, vegetable, or mineral. It was a member of the human family. But it wasn't quite normal, hence it was a life unworthy to be lived.

We have childhood euthanasia. Don't think there isn't a slippery slope. Many of us who thought the unborn were protected were horrified when the abortion mentality began to take hold and got sanction from the highest court of the land in the face of a Constitution that says no *person* shall be deprived of life, liberty, or property without due process of law nor shall any *person* be deprived of equal protection of the law. And yet seven of the judges still found a right to privacy in the

Constitution that nobody had ever seen there for 200 years that warranted exterminating the unborn constitutionally. That is what the Court did.

So that is the struggle. It is there and it is in stark terms that can't be glossed over: the quality of life ethic versus the sanctity of life ethic.

Every Life Is Precious

But I suggest to you: adopt a philosophy that says every life is precious, no matter how old, no matter how handicapped, no matter how poor, no matter how sick—no matter *anything*. Every life is precious and ought to be cherished and saved and nourished. Every life, especially the handicapped, adds to the gross spiritual product.

But with the quality of life ethic you are setting up a policy that ratifies what the Nazis did: one group of people deciding that another person or group of people is unworthy to live. The bell will toll indeed for you someday—it might very well—but you have already diminished humanity. The quality of life ethic turns John Donne on his head. He wrote, "Every man's death diminishes me because I am a part of mankind." The quality of life ethic says every man's birth diminishes me because there just isn't enough life to go around.

Abortionists Indicted

In the little courtroom of my mind I have indicted proabortionists on a three-count indictment.

The first one is that they are guilty of excessive simplicity. They think that the human problems—and God knows there are human problems with unwanted pregnancies—can be eliminated by eliminating the people. How simple! You can get rid of poverty, you can get rid of everything: just get rid of the people that are troublesome. There are too many of *those* people. There are too many people on welfare, there are too many people who are crippled and who are handicapped, too many people who are a burden to society; so the simple way, the direct way, the fastest way, is to get rid of people.

That's really their answer. Then they give you the money argument—how much it costs to bring a child into the world and how much better that that child be exterminated. (Notice they use the word *terminate* a pregnancy. Every pregnancy terminates at the end of nine months. What they mean is *exterminate* a pregnancy.)

The euphemisms are absurdly amusing. Prochoice: everyone's for choice—that sounds like freedom and the "Battle Hymn of the Republic." But what is the choice? Choice to have a baby or not? When you are pregnant you *have* a baby. Do you permit the baby to live or do you exterminate that child as a diseased appendix or an abcessed tooth? That's what they are talking about.

A Crushing Pessimism

The second count of my indictment is that these people who opt for abortion are guilty of a crushing pessimism. What a pessimism they live under, if you can call that living. They look at the down side of everything. That if you are born in a ghetto, if you are born handicapped, if you are born retarded, you haven't got a chance; life is really not worth living. They haven't got the slightest notion of the enormously great things that can happen from people despite the fact that they are born physically or mentally challenged.

My favorite story concerns Beethoven. I learned about this watching the Ninth Symphony performed on public television; the conductor told the story of Beethoven, who was stone-deaf and whose mind was failing—and he knew it—scribbling out madly his Ninth Symphony before he died or before the light went out in his mind. Then on May 7, 1824, he conducted the premiere performance in the Vienna Opera House. I can see Beethoven standing there in front of the orchestra, not hearing a note. The entire audience was in tears and cheering at the end. One of the musicians had to turn the composer around to face the audience so he could see what he couldn't hear.

The Lesson of the Crucifix

The most useful person I ever met was a thirty-two-year-old man, an inmate of Gateway House in Chicago for hardcore heroin addicts. I said to him: "When's the last time you shot up?"

He said, "Four years ago."

I said, "What turned you around?"

He said, "I've been an addict since I was fourteen and one night my friends thought I had overdosed and took me in an alley and shoved me in a garbage can and left me there. They thought I'd died.

"I came to, I realized where I was. And I said, 'I'm not garbage.' I crawled out of there and I came here. I can't read, I can't write, I clean up mostly. But what I do is, I show these dudes if a guy like me can kick it, they can kick it."

And I thought to myself: Here is an illiterate, literally human garbage, unwanted, rejected, stuffed into a garbage can. Talk about being unwanted—but how useful the life he leads giving hope to the hopeless, the most hopeless of God's creatures, the hardcore heroin addict who's got this monkey on his back. He needs hope, he needs to know it can be done. And here is this human reject showing him: "I beat it, I beat it, you can."

No psychiatrist charging $500 an hour on Park Avenue does more for his fellow human beings than that illiterate person.

And that's the lesson of the crucifix. It isn't being loved that counts; St. Francis tells us that. It's loving.

I Won't Give Up

Do you know what the suicide rate is among handicapped people? Virtually zero. They don't kill themselves. It's the beautiful people, the people who have too much of the world, too much of the attention and the adulation and the wealth and the beauty and the jet-setters. They are the ones who weary of the world. Not so the handicapped.

Greg Wittine. Twenty-three years old; Rochester, New York. Cerebral paralytic. Sits in a wheelchair. Can't talk. You'd think he was retarded; has little control over his musculature; points to the letters of an alphabet to communicate.

I watched him on television become an Eagle Scout. His chest was covered with merit badges. On the best day I ever lived, I couldn't have earned 10 percent of those merit badges. Hike ten miles? He crawled one mile and then pushed his wheelchair the other nine.

Do we need people like Greg Wittine? When we get so weary, when we think that God has forgotten us, when we think that life is not the way it ought to be and we're put upon and we're bored and we're depressed and we feel sorry for ourselves—then we think of somebody like Greg Wittine.

If you deny the existence of the human soul, then you have a responsibility to define the celestial fire in Greg Wittine who says: "I won't give up. I won't surrender to my handicaps. I'm going to achieve. I'm going to do the best I can with what God has given me."

Don't Be Pessimistic

Terry Wyles. His mother took thalidomide. He was born without arms, without legs, with one eye, and abandoned in an alley in London. This little grotesquerie, this little monster, was abandoned in an alley and picked up by the police and taken to a home run by an eccentric Englishwoman and called "The Guild of the Brave Poor Things."

Terry Wyles, at age ten, was adopted by two of the greatest losers in history: an English woman who was on her third husband, whose own children had been taken away from her by the courts (she had been adjudicated unfit). Her husband was an unemployed wounded army veteran. This couple of losers was permitted to adopt this little loser.

So Terry Wyles and his new family came together. Terry Wyles is a journalist today. He has written a book called *On the Shoulders of Giants.* His father became an electronics wizard and developed a chair that he could move up and down and control. Prince Philip has visited the family several times.

Don't ever think that because you have very humble beginnings, very tragic beginnings, that there isn't hope there. Ethel Waters, the great entertainer who died recently, wrote a book, *His Eye Is on the Sparrow,* restating the obvious. In it she said: "My father raped my mother when she was twelve and, you know what, they're dedicating a park to me in Lancaster, Pennsylvania."

Proabortionists Lack Imagination

The third count of my indictment on the proabortionists is: They lack imagination. What a terrible thing not to know, not to understand the dimensions of what they are doing.

They don't understand that of these little lives that they are throwing away, that they are exterminating rivers to be crossed and books to be written and secrets to be discovered and cures to be developed; songs and poems and so much to be done that will not be done. And they are getting in the way by exterminating these little human lives.

I suppose their lack of imagination preserves their sanity. F. Scott Fitzgerald said: "In the dark night of the soul, it's always 3:00 A.M." And I suppose at 3:00 A.M. in their souls, if they ever wake up and try to think of the dimensions of what they are doing, of what they are accessories to. . . . I think it preserves their sanity that they lack the imagination to understand what they are doing.

Much Is Expected of You

I want to communicate to you that you have a double burden. You have been blessed with so much. But you can't get out of it that easily. Much is expected of you because you have been given so much here.

I hope that you will never be discouraged. I hope you will never be cynical because no cathedral was ever built by cynics. You can't be cynical. Simple as a dove, wise as a serpent—but that doesn't mean cynical.

Henry Adams described the cathedral at Chartres as embodying the noblest aspirations of mankind, the reaching up to infinity. I suggest to you that the prolife movement is like that because it has no self-interest.

People in the prolife movement are not fighting for longer vacation or better pay or better working conditions. They are fighting for a lot of little people they'll never see and never know, loving people who can't love back.

That's unique and that's what makes it great. Harry Emerson Fosdick said, "We can't all be great but we can belong to something that's great."

Fight for the Innocently Inconvenient

I suggest fighting for the innocently inconvenient, who can't vote, who can't rise up in the streets, who can't escape. And indeed—in the words I just heard when I was presented this beautiful medal—"whatsoever you do for the least of these you do unto Me."

I have been in the refugee camps in Thailand; I have been in the refugee camps in Malaysia; and I have seen what I thought were the least of God's creatures, the refugees from Cambodia and from Vietnam who would rather die than live under those conditions. They are fleeing from a sort of peace. They are fleeing from the evil peace of the prison and the graveyard.

I thought surely these people are the least of God's creatures but I was quite wrong. They have legs to run with, and voices to cry with, and eyes to weep with. The unborn are the least of God's creatures. We know that what we do for them we do unto him.

The Sins of Omission

Let me close by just suggesting a little sadness on my part when I think of my age. I have used up so many years of whatever time God has allotted me. I've used up most of it.

So think of yourself in terms of the time that you have been allotted and what you must do with it, that you really haven't the luxury of not putting it to the utmost use.

I believe, speaking for the prolife people, that when the final judgment comes—as it will surely—when that moment comes that you face Almighty God—the individual judgment, the particular judgment—I believe that a terror will grip your soul like none other you can imagine. The sins of omission will be what weigh you down; not the things you've done wrong, the chances you've taken, but the things you failed to do, the times that you stepped back, the times you didn't speak out.

Not only for every idle word but for every idle silence must man render an account. I think that you will be overwhelmed with remorse for the things you failed to do.

The Voices Never Heard in This World

But I do believe that people in the prolife movement will hear voices on their behalf advocating Christ's mercy. I think they will hear little voices that were never heard in this world but are heard in the next world in a chorus like Handel's

Messiah saying: "Forgive him, forgive him, he loved us very much."

I believe the terror that you will feel at that time, if you work for the unborn, will be lifted when you hear the words: "Come, beloved of my Father and enter the kingdom."

I congratulate you, I envy you, and I hope today is only the commencement.

SIX

Priestly Peacemakers: The Bishops and Nuclear Strategy

On May 3, 1983, the Catholic bishops of the United States, with only nine dissenting votes, approved their now-famous pastoral letter "The Challenge of Peace." Two earlier drafts had been circulated for comment by interested parties. Comment was forthcoming—in abundance. Many praised the bishops for their moral courage in speaking out on the subject of nuclear weapons. Others expressed reservations. Many Catholics perceived a naivete toward the Soviet threat and a drift toward pacifism in the pastoral letter.

Among those who reacted with energy if not enthusiasm to the second draft of the letter was a group of Catholic members of Congress. I drafted a letter summarizing our misgivings and submitted it to as many Catholic members of Congress as I could encounter in a day and a half during a special session of Congress in December, 1982. I approached twenty-four members; twenty-three agreed to sign the letter. One declined for political reasons. Most of those signing were Republicans because I am a Republican and am obviously more comfortable talking to my fellow Republicans. But two signatories are Democrats, and I am confident that I could have gained the signatures of many more Catholic Congressmen, both Republican and Democrat, if I had had more time.

The third and final draft of the pastoral letter made some changes that were suggested in our letter. I do not claim that our letter moved the bishops off any particular position; I only note that we were critical of some aspects of the second draft that did not appear in the final document. One change particularly comes to mind. The second draft contained a statement that the power of nuclear weapons "threatens the sovereignty of God" over his creation. We doubt that mere creatures can threaten God's sovereignty. I noted with some small pleasure that this statement was not included in the last draft of the pastoral.

The thrust of our misgivings about the pastoral, however, still applies to the final draft. I noted the very telling remark of the archbishop of Paris who commented that the pacifism of the American bishops is that of people who know that nothing will ever happen to them. The U.S. bishops are far removed in years, geography, and understanding from the Soviet threat.

The letter is addressed to Archbishop Joseph Bernardin of Chicago, chairman of the committee that drafted the letter. The text follows:

DEAR ARCHBISHOP BERNARDIN:

As Catholic members of the United States Congress, we feel a profound responsibility for the direction of our nation's defense policy. As laymen, we are responsible for the concrete application of moral principles, and we are grateful for the spiritual guidance provided by our common faith. Naturally, then, we have a unique stake in the success of the National Conference of Catholic Bishops in its preparation of the Pastoral Letter on War and Peace.

However, from our perspective as legislators, we see a number of difficulties with the draft version of that Pastoral Letter which has been made public by the U.S. Catholic Conference. Precisely because we are so interested in the success of that endeavor, we hope that you will take into account our thoughts on this difficult issue.

We are ever mindful that lawmakers, sworn to uphold the

public trust, have a sacred duty to protect the people they represent. Pope John XXIII emphasized this obligation in his great encyclical *Pacem in Terris,* echoing the words of Pope Leo XIII, "that the safety of the commonwealth is not only the first law, but is a government's whole reason for existence." The preamble to the Constitution we are sworn to uphold asserts as among its primary purposes to "provide for the common defense" and additionally, to "secure the blessing of liberty to ourselves and our posterity."

That special calling gives us a special perspective on the question of national defense, and prompts our reflections on the draft Pastoral Letter. We can divide our concerns into five categories, as follows:

1. The Nature of the Soviet Threat

Our national defense posture—especially insofar as it involves nuclear weapons—is poised to counter the very real threat of Soviet communism. The tensions generated by Soviet expansionism cause the greatest fears of war. Without a threat from the Soviet Union, there would be no arms race. But the policies of our adversary have made the arms race inevitable. In recent years, the Soviet government has undertaken the greatest arms build-up in history. And the historical record compiled by the Soviet leadership gives us every reason to suspect that, if we let our defenses lag, we will pay an enormous price in lost human liberties—not only for ourselves but for free people everywhere.

Pope Pius XII instructed us that "there are human goods of so high an order that immense sacrifices may have to be borne in their defense." Among those human goods are the rights to liberty and to freedom of conscience—rights that are crushed under communist regimes. The Connecticut Conference of Bishops has made the point succinctly: "In view of its proven record, Communism now actively threatens the existence of all religions and of all places of worship in the world." We cannot, in good conscience, allow the degradation of God-given human rights—in our own country or in the countries that depend upon our support for their liberty. We think it worth knowing that after the communist coup in Afghanistan, the loyalty of Afghan officers was tested by the demand—under pain of death—that they walk on the Koran.

History also teaches us, quite clearly, that the Soviet government will take advantage of any lapses in the defense of the free world. In Hungary, in Czechoslovakia, and now in Afghanistan, the Soviets have demonstrated their aggressive intentions.

In short, our real threat is not embodied in weapons—however gruesome modern weaponry might become. Our real threat comes from an ideology that challenges our fundamental faith in human dignity. As Father John Courtney Murray pointed out:

> Only Soviet doctrine makes Soviet power a threat to the United States. Only Soviet doctrine explains the peculiar nature of Soviet imperialism and shows it to be unappeasable in its new dynamism. Only Soviet doctrine illuminates the intentions of the new messianism that has come out of the East, fitted with the armature of power, and organized implacably against the West.

2. The Nature of Contemporary Warfare

The threat of a full-scale nuclear war arouses the greatest possible fears in modern society, and secular commentators invoke an apocalyptic vision of modern warfare. But for most of the people in the world today, the greatest danger of war still involves conventional weapons. Since World War II there have been hundreds of conventional wars, local insurrections, border conflicts, and guerrilla attacks; the death toll from this warfare runs into the tens of millions.

To date, despite years of international tensions, none of those smaller battles has escalated into a world conflagration. Although we have never truly seen peace, we have at least seen limitations on wars. Those limitations are imposed largely by the strength of the U.S. defense posture, which denies aggressors the prospect of an easy victory. Our defenses deter conventional attacks, sparing untold human tragedy, by imposing risks on potential aggressors. Given the nature of our adversary, there is no other way to stave off violence. "But if there is no risk," Father Murray concluded, "or only a minimal risk, aggressive policies will be carried through, as they were in Hungary, where nothing was done to create a risk."

Particularly in Western Europe, where recent generations have seen so much bloodshed, the Soviet Union has an awesome preponderance of conventional weaponry. Only our nuclear deterrent force inhibits the Soviets from using that advantage to intimidate our allies on that continent.

In view of these strategic realities, our nuclear deterrent force should be seen not as a threat to peace, but as a guarantor of peace. A capable, flexible defense posture allows us to deter war and spare human lives in two different but related ways. First, we prevent the occurrence of some wars of aggression. Second, and equally important, when war does break out we limit it as much as possible to local, conventional conflict.

Since we cannot entirely eliminate the possibility of war, our goal as legislators is to create a national defense that could hold warfare in check. If war does break out we must bring the fighting quickly to a halt. To accomplish this objective, we must have weapons that can be used quickly, efficiently, and discriminately to halt aggression.

We do not wish to enter into a discussion of whether or not a limited nuclear war is possible, because the answer to this controversy is not essential to our general position. We do encourage, nevertheless, research and development of new and more discriminate weapons—whether nuclear or conventional—that can more precisely target military as opposed to civilian targets.

As the bishops judge the morality of nuclear weapons, we ask that they consider that conventional weapons can indeed impose levels of destruction that may be indistinguishable from nuclear weapons, as Dresden, Tokyo and Coventry bear witness. From the perspective of the survivors of Hiroshima or Dresden, the bombing strategy was at least as crucial as the type and number of weapons used.

Our nuclear deterrent is designed to preserve the peace by offsetting Soviet nuclear and massive conventional military forces. Thus should we dismantle our nuclear deterrent we actually increase the danger of war, whether conventional or nuclear.

True, as in the past, a European conventional war might spare the United States. But we recall the words of Stephen Spender, in his horror at the violence of the Spanish Civil War: "It came to me that unless I cared about every murdered child indiscriminately, I didn't really care about children being murdered at all." We cannot forsake our allies simply to allay our own fears.

3. Nuclear Strategy

The draft letter condemns any strategy that envisages the massive bombing of civilian population centers. This condemnation is clearly in line with Catholic teachings since the advent of nuclear weapons. We would only add that the documents of Vatican II are somewhat more precise when they condemn "modern scientific weapons" rather than nuclear weapons as such. Again, conventional weapons can carry out the same grisly mission.

The doctrine of Mutually Assured Destruction does indeed contemplate massive retaliatory bombing of Soviet cities, and we welcome the bishops' injunction against that policy.

However, the N.C.C.B. should be aware that American defense policy in recent years had shifted dramatically away from the MAD doctrine. Our strategic planners (under President Carter as well as President Reagan) have been moving toward a more rational nuclear posture, in which our own weapons are aimed not at Soviet cities, but at our adversary's own strategic forces. In our view, this new direction makes American policy both more effective and more moral.

However, the draft Pastoral Letter does not recognize the shift in American policy—a misunderstanding that Judge Clark has emphasized in his letter to the Bishops. Moreover, the draft Pastoral does not allow for a nuclear strategy that emphasizes "counterforce" rather than "counter-value" targeting. In fact, the draft condemns "the willingness to foster stragetic planning which seeks a nuclear war fighting capability."

If the United States did not have a nuclear war fighting capability, how could we preserve our deterrent? Deterrence depends entirely on the Soviets' perception of our ability to withstand attack. If our adversary knows that we cannot fight a nuclear war effectively, he has no reason to inhibit his own aggressive instincts. If we retain our nuclear weapons, but eliminate our strategic options for waging war, the only remaining possibility is a return to the MAD strategy—the strategy we have condemned as immoral.

Ambassador Rowny, our top negotiator in the present arms-control talks, has summarized this point quite well. Without a war fighting capability, we would limit ourselves to only one response in case of Soviet aggression. And, Ambassador Rowny observes, "there would be only one feasible target for that response—Soviet cities and their civilian population. The moral condemnation of such targeting of cities is crystal clear in the documents of Vatican II and in post-conciliar papal statements."

We have seen, in recent weeks, a great deal of debate about

the nature of the Vatican statements on nuclear weapons. We have heard many different interpretations of Pope John Paul's message to the United Nations, although the wording of that message seems clear enough to us: "In current conditions, deterrence based on balance, certainly not as an end in itself, but as a step toward progressive disarmament, may still be judged morally acceptable." We can concur, for that matter, with Cardinal Krol's amendment, substituting "tolerable" for "acceptable."

Whatever connotations different interpreters might place upon that statement, and similar statements by previous popes, we find Professor William O'Brien convincing in his explanation: "It should be clear, however, that given ample opportunity, neither the popes, including John Paul II, nor Vatican II has condemned the present deterrent and defense posture of the Free World, much less ordered the faithful to subvert or oppose them." We wholeheartedly concur without reservation in the message of our Holy Father to the United Nations, and we earnestly pray that our bishops do not reach an opposite conclusion.

4. Arms Control and the Arms Race

The history of arms control negotiations is not a happy one. Successive talks and agreements have taken very little momentum out of the arms race, and it would be difficult to find anyone who feels safer today as a result of the agreements we have concluded with the Soviet Union in past years. Nevertheless, the draft letter gives very little credit to the United States for its efforts to introduce real restraints on nuclear weaponry.

Since the first atomic bomb was invented, there has been only one serious proposal for world disarmament: the Baruch plan, which was introduced by the U.S. during a time when our nation enjoyed a nuclear monopoly. That plan, and every subsequent suggestion that included the vital element of effective verification, was rejected by the Soviet leadership.

Still, the United States government has persisted in good-faith bargaining, and today President Reagan has offered a dramatic decrease in the nuclear armament of the unstable European theatre.

Even without a comprehensive agreement to curtail the arms race, in recent years the United States has reduced substantially the number of nuclear weapons in its arsenal. As part of the 1979 NATO decision on intermediate nuclear forces, we even withdrew, unilaterally, 1,000 nuclear warheads from Europe. But these and other similar self-imposed restraints by the United States have not been matched by the USSR, which has consistently expanded its nuclear arsenal and its capability for nuclear and conventional aggression. The final Pastoral Letter should, we respectfully assert, give credit where it is due. Perhaps even more important, however, is the fact that in its present form, the draft letter does not seem to differentiate between the intent of the nuclear weapons systems deployed by the United States and the Soviet Union. As it now stands, in fact, we are condemned equally—if not more—than the Soviets for possessing huge weapons. Surely there is room for a more objective assessment of this point. The essence of our policy is, and always has been, to deter war, especially nuclear war. Our principal alliance relationship, NATO, is dedicated to preserving the values, tradition, and heritage of Western civilization—including the freedom of religious choice. It would be preposterous to characterize NATO as anything but a defensive organization which seeks to prevent an aggressor from starting a war.

Unfortunately, the Soviet Union does not share our world view. Its record on human rights and religious toleration is engraved on the bloodstained streets of Eastern Europe and Afghanistan. Its military forces—including its burgeoning nuclear strike systems—are built around the concept of the offensive. The unprecedented size and scope of their aggressive capabilities should warn us against repeating the tragic mistakes of the 1930s, when the West, in attempting to project a policy of peace at all costs, actually emboldened the fascist dictators to embark upon the aggressive steps which resulted in the Second World War. We recall that following Pearl Harbor draftees were drilling in Grant Park, Chicago, with broom handles instead of rifles. The margin for error we once had no longer exists.

We are far from unanimous concerning the funding for production of the MX missile. Even so, we recognize that it is designed to correct an imbalance between our present defense posture and the Soviet's first-strike ICBM capability. All of us hope that should production of this weapon go forward, it will provide an incentive to the Soviets to negotiate significant strategic reductions.

How can we create that possibility, without increasing the risks of general warfare? New advances in technology have raised exciting possibilities for defensive systems that might take away the advantage of a nuclear first strike. Anti-missile defenses of varying description have been proposed, including some that promise a comprehensive cover against a first strike. If they are successfully developed, such defenses could help to eliminate the moral quandary of nuclear deterrence. We cannot yet be certain that such defensive systems will succeed, but we can at least be open to that possibility. In particular, in considering the Pastoral Letter on War and Peace, the bishops should contemplate the possibility that nuclear devices might be constructed for solely defensive purposes. Surely such devices could not fall under the condemnation of nuclear weapons in the draft letter.

5. The Road toward Peace

As legislators operating in an imperfect world, we cannot hope to eliminate all conflicts among nations. As Christians, we look forward to the reconciliation of all men in Jesus, but we recognize that such reconciliation will not come about as a result of our inadequate efforts. Therefore, we join our spiritual leaders in calling for prayer for peace. We cannot, and should not, attempt to solve all our problems without invoking the Lord's help.

However, we can and should address the root causes of the tension that currently plagues the world. We can fight against violence without resorting to violence, by refusing to allow the degradation of human rights around the world. As representatives of the free world, we must emphasize the truth about human nature and human freedom—the "unalienable rights" on which our republic is founded. Aleksandr Solzhenitsyn has come to us as a spiritual witness to the corrupt ideology against which we must do battle. Lies cause violence, Solzhenitsyn tells us, and to avoid violence we must do homage to the truth. We are fighting a battle of ideas daily—a battle as important as any other we might face.

As the N.C.C.B. continues its discussion on the Pastoral Letter, we urge all the bishops to keep this spiritual battle in mind. No true peace is possible unless human dignity is upheld. The crisis we face today does not involve two morally equal forces, but the contention of human freedom against totalitarianism. As Pope John Paul II wrote in *Redemptor Hominis,* "After all, peace comes down to respect for man's inviolable rights."

Forgive us if we speak too bluntly, but we do so because we take your Excellencies' efforts with the utmost gravity and respect. But we would expect the view that no values are worth defending if a nuclear war might ensue to be espoused by materialists—those who are at best agnostic about the existence of the immortal soul and the nature of good and evil. When we read such pessimism from some of our bishops who are dedicated to the propagation of the faith, we cannot but wonder, "What faith?"

In all the burgeoning literature of apocalypse surrounding this issue we have never encountered such a startling statement as the second draft contains, when it says: "Today the destructive potential of the nuclear powers threatens the sovereignty of God over the world He has brought into being. We could destroy His work." The notion that mere creatures could do anything to "threaten the sovereignty of God over the world" strikes us as one definition of Original Sin.

We would hope that those who would disarm us in the name of peace might dwell more deeply on their responsibility for the moral character of the peace that would follow our surrender. Peace without justice is moral violence. The boat people of Vietnam aren't fleeing a war, they are fleeing a peace without justice. We do not see capitulation to evil as an act of morality, nor do we believe that survival is the only value worth preserving. Of course we do not attribute a contrary view to you nor the Conference, but simply want to share with you the depth of our convictions.

We cannot accept the notion implicit in some interpretations of the morality of nuclear deterrence that our only Catholic President, John F. Kennedy, was less that moral in defending our freedom during the Cuban missile crisis of 1962. We recall his report to the American people on radio and television October 22, 1962, when he said:

> Our policy has been one of patience and restraint, as befits a peaceful and powerful nation, which leads a worldwide alliance . . . .But now further action is required—and it is under way; and these actions may only be the beginning. We will not prematurely or unnecessarily risk the costs of worldwide nuclear war in which even the fruits of victory would be ashes in our mouth—but neither will we shrink from that risk at any time it must be faced.

We take a special pride in President Kennedy's ringing conclusion:

> The path we have chosen for the present is full of hazards, as all paths are—but it is the one most consistent with our character and courage as a nation and our commitments around the world. The cost of freedom is always high—but

Americans have always paid it. And one path we shall never choose, and that is the path of surrender or submission.

Our goal is not the victory of might, but the vindication of right—not peace at the expense of freedom, but both peace *and* freedom, here in this hemisphere, and, we hope, around the world. God willing, that goal will be achieved.

Once again, we hope that the bishops will consider these thoughts from laymen who, like themselves, are caught up in the horrible dilemmas posed by nuclear weaponry. Our hopes and prayers are with you as you enter the final phase of your debate.

Sincerely,

Charles F. Dougherty, *Pennsylvania*
Robert K. Dornan, *California*
James L. Nelligan, *Pennsylvania*
William Carney, *New York*
Eldon Rudd, *Arizona*
Joe Skeen, *New Mexico*
George Wortley, *New York*
Guy Molinari, *New York*
Edward Madigan, *Illinois*
Manuel Lujan, Jr., *New Mexico*
Bill Lowery, *California*
Billy Tauzin, *Louisiana*
Henry J. Hyde, *Illinois*
Daniel A. Lungren, *California*
E. Clay Shaw, Jr., *Florida*
Vin Weber, *Minnesota*
Ray McGrath, *New York*
John Erlenborn, *Illinois*
Thomas Hartnett, *South Carolina*
Edward Derwinski, *Illinois*
Tom Corcoran, *Illinois*
John Hiler, *Indiana*
Gene Chappie, *California*
John Breaux, *Louisiana*

SEVEN

Some Thoughts on Liberation Theology

B EFORE HE WAS BEHEADED, St. Thomas More said: "I die the king's good servant, but God's first." The great English statesman had his priorities straight. He obeyed Jesus' command to "render therefore unto Caesar the things that are Caesar's; and unto God the things that are God's." More served Caesar well, withholding his first loyalty, knowing that serving Caesar was not the most important thing.

If he were alive today, Thomas More would have been able to see right to the heart of the flaws of liberation theology, the influential movement that once again confuses the things of Caesar with the things of God.

Liberation theology forcibly merges religion and politics. It accomplishes this feat by reinterpreting the Gospels in an effort to reconcile Marx with Christ. Liberation theologians make the audacious claim that the Christian and Marxist views of mankind are compatible, if not identical.

Liberation theology has profound foreign policy implications for the United States. Religiously inspired revolutions can be formidable, as we have seen in the Middle East. Despite their many dissimilarities, both Khomeini Islamic fundamentalists and liberation theologians see the United States as "the Great Satan"—the source of evil in today's world. Both sanction violent acts to deal with that evil.

Traditional Marxism opposed the Church head on: Lenin's most famous utterance was "religion is the opium of the people." In some areas of the world, however, people's devotion to religion is too deeply ingrained to easily eradicate, and so a new "theology of liberation" has appeared. This development does not so much oppose religion as use it in moving toward the same end—the triumph of Marxism. The gospels are not rejected; they are reinterpreted to satisfy the demands of Marxist analysis.

In Latin America, the liberation theologians combine the indigenous Catholic religious traditions of the campesinos with the hope of economic transformation that, the liberation theologians claim, is realizable here and now, not in the after-life. They identify capitalism and free enterprise with the Protestant ethic of economic individualism, which they regard as unacceptable.

Let liberation theologians speak for themselves:

I consider Fidel Castro to be a person inspired and led by the Holy Spirit. I liked it when Fidel went to Chile and told the priests that in Latin America the alliance between Marxists and Christian revolutionaries is not a tactical, but a strategic alliance, that is not temporary, but permanent and necessary. Also, I like the saying of Ché Guevara (another Marxist saint, who gave his life for the poor, guided by the Spirit of Jesus without knowing him) that "when the Christians in Latin America take seriously the revolutionary teachings of the gospel, the revolution will be invincible."

Those provocative words are taken from *To Be a Revolutionary*, the autobiography of Padre J. Guadalupe Carney, an American-born priest, who is believed to have starved to death in 1983 while in the company of Cuban trained guerrillas in Honduras. The book was published in 1985 by Harper and Row, a leading U.S. publisher.

Equally revealing are these comments from *A Theology of Liberation* (Orbis, 1984) by Fr. Gustavo Gutierrez, a Peruvian Jesuit who is generally acknowledged as the founder of liberation theology:

> The building of a just society means the confrontation—in which different kinds of violence are present—between groups with different interests and opinions. . . .Participation in the process of liberation is an obligatory and privileged *locus* for Christian life and reflection. . . .To characterize Latin America as a dominated and oppressed continent naturally leads one to speak of liberation and above all to participate in the process. . . .Among more alert groups today. . . a new awareness of Latin American reality is making headway. They believe that there can be authentic development for Latin America only if there is liberation from the domination exercised by the great capitalist countries, and especially the most powerful, the United States of America. . . . Moreover, it is becoming more obvious that the revolutionary process ought to embrace the whole continent. There is little chance of success for attempts limited to a national scope.

In his autobiography, Fr. Carney makes it plain that his intention is to convince Christians that Christianity and Marxism are compatible:

> I invite all Christians who read this to get rid of any unfair and un-Christian prejudices you have against armed revolutions, socialism, Marxism, and communism. I would hope that this book has helped you get rid of any mental blocks that you might have because of capitalist propaganda

and a false, bourgeois version of Christianity that has been put into your heads since childbirth. There is no contradiction whatsoever between being a Christian and a priest, and being a Marxist revolutionary.

Fr. Ernesto Cardenal, Sandinista Minister of Culture in Nicaragua, said it bluntly: "Christians are not only able to be Marxists but, on the contrary, to be authentically Christian, they ought to be Marxists." He explains:

Our only solution is Marxism. It is the only possible way to achieve freedom. I do not see any other course we can take if the promises of history and of the gospel are going to become true. There is no salvation outside the Church, and there is no liberation outside Marxism; that is why I preach both. For me, the revolution and the kingdom of heaven, mentioned in the gospel, are the same thing. A Christian should embrace Marxism if he wants to be with God and all men.

These are not mere speculations by Latin American theologians and revolutionaries. Liberation theology has serious consequences. It exercises real influence over the imagination of Christians in this hemisphere. However, liberation theology is bad religion and bad politics. Liberation theologians are naive about the nature of man and the nature of Marxism. If they succeed in merging religion and politics as they want to do, they will not liberate people, but rather bring them into a new and more suffocating bondage than the world has ever known.

Let us first consider the religious content of liberation theology.

Criticism of liberation theology from within the Catholic Church has focused on the inherent contradiction of wedding Christianity with Marxism. Cardinal Obando y Bravo of Nicaragua and Archbishop Rivera y Damas of El Salvador have been particularly outspoken on this point as they have worked tirelessly to separate the Church's social justice agenda from endorsement of leftist revolution.

Cardinal Obando y Bravo knows liberation theology up close. He had high hopes for it at first, but now sees what it really involves. "I thought liberation theology could help people and could play a role in reducing the enormous gap between rich and poor," he said. "But now, watching it in practice, I think this is unlikely because I see that it foments class hatred."

Archbishop John Quinn of San Francisco, a leading American prelate with close ties to Latin America, points out the fundamental conflict between Marxism and Christianity. Marxism, he says, "presents class hatred and the class struggle as a fundamental postulate of human liberation" which is "incompatible with the Gospel whose first commandment is love."

Pope John Paul II knows about Communism too. In 1984, the Pope approved a Vatican instruction about liberation theology prepared by Cardinal Joseph Ratzinger, prefect of the Congregation of the Doctrine of the Faith, and Archbishop Alberto Bovone. This document put its finger on the essential problem:

Atheism and the denial of the human person, his liberty and his rights, are at the core of Marxist theory. This theory then contains errors which directly threaten the truths of the faith regarding the eternal destiny of individual persons. Moreover, to attempt to integrate into theology an analysis whose criterion of interpretation depends on this atheistic conception is to involve oneself in terrible contradictions. What is more, this misunderstanding of the spiritual nature of the person leads to a total subordination of the person to the collectivity and thus to the denial of the principles of a social and political life which is in keeping with human dignity.

The philosophy of Marx excludes a spiritual realm. History, Marx declared, unfolds according to the immutable law of the process of dialectical materialism. "Dialectical" means that every entity begets its opposite, and the entities, classes, or societies inevitably conflict. Out of this conflict the original entities become submerged into a new entity which then proceeds to beget its opposite. And so the dialectical process unfolds.

The key word is *process*, proceeding rigidly, mechanically, not through chance or circⁱ stance, but according to immutable laws of thesis, antithesis, and synthesis. Marxist philosophy is materialistic. Marxists believe in no spiritual realm, no immortⁱl soul, and hence no sin and no salvation. People in the Marxist system are no more than units of production and consumption. The only reality is material. Hence religion is dangerous folly in theory as well as in practice. Lenin once said, "We must fight religion," and the tyrants who have followed him in power all over the world have done precisely that.

It is thus astonishing to find priests who declare themselves to be Marxists. "Marxist priests," the exponents of liberation theology, constitute a perfect oxymoron, no less contradictory than a "carnivorous vegetarian."

This is not to deny the idealism of many priests who identify themselves with liberation theology out of a sincere desire to change the social and economic environment in which they find themselves. They see grinding poverty all around them. They question the systems that allow such conditions to exist. They work for justice. For many, however, economic justice becomes a more important virtue than charity.

This leads to a confusion of priorities. We need to heed Christ's command in the Gospel of Saint Matthew: render to Caesar the things that are Caesar's and to God the things that are God's. As Thomas More knew, the things that are God's come first.

I think we need to look at God's side of the equation. Have we gotten out of balance? Has our concern for social and economic justice, justified as it is, become so overpowering that the message of the church is reduced from the spiritual level to that of political and social action?

J. Brian Benestad of the University of Scranton has written a thoughtful study of this question, *The Pursuit of a Just Social Order*. He agrees that working for economic and social development and the protection of human rights is important and necessary. But Dr. Benestad also points out the limitations of this kind of work from a spiritual point of view: these are worthy goals, but their attainment by the people of a nation does not directly lead to conversion of its citizens. Persons who have sufficient material goods and socioeconomic, political and civil rights may be atheists, or may simply be dedicated to their own self-interest. In other words, justice as it is popularly understood today does not imply transformation in the individual soul. Ought not the transformation of souls be the chief task of the church?

The transformation of souls is what God desires. The transformation of our own soul is of eternal importance to each of us. When a Christian considers what is good for the world, surely we would put highest priority on guarantees of religious freedom, so that all men and women can respond to God's invitation to know him and be saved.

The triumph of Marxism, however, means the end of religious freedom. Marxist Christians in Latin America should look at those communist countries where the Marxists have had enough time to consolidate their power. In the Soviet Union, Czechoslovakia, Poland, and other communist countries, overt hostility to religion is a feature of the Marxist system.

Religion, as the institutional acknowledgement of man's relationship to God, is the indispensable underpinning for human dignity. That is why religious freedom is a basic human right. That is why Marxists, when they strip away religious freedom, are attacking the very basis of human dignity.

Finally, we have every reason to be skeptical about the economic and political program that the liberation theologians would impose after the revolution. To replace a dictatorship of the right with one on the left—as has been done in Cuba and Nicaragua—delivers yet one more version of late twentieth century serfdom, a serfdom in which the state owns both body and soul. In 1984, Polish writers associated with the Solidarity trade union movement said as much in a letter to Nicaragua's Fr. Cardenal. The writers said: "We know all too well the abuses inflicted on the idea of freedom, and the people who believed in it and fought for it. On the basis of our experience we cannot recognize the purity of intentions of those who hold the banner of freedom but cooperate with the cruelest slave empire in history."

Michael Novak puts it succinctly when he points out that liberation theology lacks a concrete vision of political economy: "It refuses to say how safeguards for human rights, economic development, and personal liberties will be instituted after the revolution. Liberation theology appears to trust its own fervent Christianity as a sufficient brake on tyranny. This is naivete—already unmasked in Nicaragua." Citing estimates of a projected need of some 76 million new jobs in Latin America by 1999, Novak comments that:

> Revolutionaries in Cuba, Nicaragua, and Vietnam, among other communist countries, mostly create huge armies. Only economic activists create jobs. Sooner or later, liberation theologies will need to grapple with how new wealth can be created and sustained systematically.

In summary, liberation theology's impact on Latin American and American politics has presented those who shape U.S. foreign policy with an imminent challenge that must be met head on. This means engaging in public dialogue and debate with the "liberationists" at every opportunity with the objective of informing both U.S. and foreign audiences of the theology's shortcomings.

It also means demonstrating that the U.S. model is worth

imitating. It is clear that the system in the United States is awesomely successful in creating jobs and wealth. We should also demonstrate our success in administering justice and defending human dignity.

If preserving human rights is the test of a government, how does the United States measure up? This is a question that invites overstatement. Some will say that the United States has gone around the world doing God's work. Others will say that America is a great enemy of human rights and freedom. I do not claim that the United States is a perfect secular state, but I think we have done well in these matters. We have objective standards to guide us: equal protection of the law and due process at home, and a commitment to freedom and democracy that has been tested in two World Wars and other protracted conflicts in Asia. We should make this case strongly, to everyone who is sincerely concerned about justice and human dignity.

We should also talk to the liberation theologians themselves. Because they have not thought much about what happens in the post-revolutionary period, I would like to think that we can disabuse at least the majority of them of their anti-U.S. notions and make them realize that this country's system is not the problem but the solution. In view of what is at stake, we have no time to lose.